Breaking Bread
in Galilee

BREAKING BREAD
IN GALILEE

A Culinary Journey into
the Promised Land

Abbie Rosner

Hilayon Press

Israel

www.galileecuisine.co.il

Published by Hilayon Press

Israel

www.hilayonpress.com

ISBN: 978-965-7594-00-1

Cover and author photograph: Tal Gluck

Book design: Longfeather Book Design

For Ron

Chronological Note: In the broadest of strokes, and without jumping into the fray, the context for the narratives of the Hebrew Bible is the ancient Near East, covering a period spanning the Late Bronze and Iron Ages—from the early second millennium to the 2nd century BCE.

Acknowledgements

This book is a celebration of exceptional friendship and sharing, and my gratitude knows no bounds. In addition to the people who grace its pages, I would like to thank the Abassi family, Yossi Ben-Artzi, Reuven Berger, Motzi Betzer, Eli Cohen, Elissa Y. Cohen, David Eitam, Yossi Garfinkel, Arnon Golan, Darra Goldstein, Amin Suleiman Hassan, Catherine Ivry, Lisa Kaftori, Erez Komarovsky, Hadas Lahav, Ronit Maoz, Uri Meyer-Chissik, Dani Nadel, Mahmoud and Nuzha Nassar, Haim Nerson, Nimmer Nimmer, Sarit Regev, Mark and Amira Rubin, Marlene Schoofs, Meir and Rina Shalev, Eyal Shapira, Miryam Sivan, Yoram Steinberger, Avi Tsiterspieler, Dina Yogev, Dahlia Zaguri, and The Havura, among many others whose names I have regrettably but unintentionally omitted. Thanks also to my parents, sisters and friends who read the manuscript at different stages, as it evolved from shoot to bud, from flower to fruit. Special thanks to Steven Bauer, Susan Weingarten and Lillian Klein Abensohn, for their thoughtful reading.

Table of Contents

For the Lord your God is bringing you into a good land,
a land with streams and springs and fountains issuing from plain and
hill; a land of wheat and barley, of vines, figs and pomegranates,
a land of olive trees and honey; a land where you may eat food without
stint, where you will lack nothing... Deuteronomy 8:7-9

And so
it has taken me
all of sixty years
to understand
that water is the finest drink,
and bread the most delicious food,
and that art is worthless
unless it plants
a measure of splendor in people's hearts.

After we die
and the weary heart
has lowered its final eyelid
on all that we've done,
and on all that we've longed for,
on all that we've dreamt of,
all we've desired
or felt,
hate will be
the first thing
to putrefy
within us.

Taha Muhammad Ali
translated by Peter Cole, Yahya Hijazi, and Gabriel Levin

Introduction

A land of wheat and barley, of vines, figs and pomegranates,
a land of olives and honey... Deuteronomy 8:8

Millennia have passed since this depiction of the Promised Land was recorded, and still I find that it eloquently describes the agricultural landscape of my Galilee home. Summer through fall, we gather figs, pomegranates and olives from trees in our yard, their seasons gracefully segueing one into the other. Wheat and barley in both wild and cultivated varieties blanket the surrounding fields, ripening from winter emerald to spring harvest gold. And dates, the probable origin of this particular biblical reference to honey, bunch in sticky caramel clusters in the fronds of a neighbor's palm tree.

In the late 1980s I moved to Alonei Aba, a small farming village in the Jezreel Valley region of the Lower Galilee, trading American city life for a new language, a foreign culture and a handsome dairy-farmer husband. What I received in the bargain was a foothold in a land that would capture my imagination and my heart.

For a city girl, one of the most intriguing aspects of life on a farm was the proximity to food at its source. After work, my husband Ron would return from the dairy, depositing a pile of rank clothes by the washing machine and an aluminum container of fresh milk on the counter for me to strain and boil—the thick upper layer of cream saved for our afternoon coffee. On our long walks in the surrounding fields I became increasingly aware of the changing of the seasons according to what was growing on either side of the path, and whether it was ripe for eating.

In the first heat-drenched days of spring, we would pick sunny orange loquats off the trees, sucking the tart flesh and spitting out the shiny brown seeds. By summer, Muscat table grapes from the village vineyard were our dessert, and we stalked the vines to glean the tiny clusters left behind by the pickers. In fall, we would stake out several olive trees of the favored "Suri" variety, and fill our pails before going home to crack each fruit with a rock, then deposit it in a jar to be cured. Most novel of all, though, for a former Eastcoaster, was the mild, rainy winter that heralded a profusion of fertility and good eating. Everywhere the citrus trees drooped with fruit, and I discovered thick-skinned pomelos, so much sweeter and more coarsely textured than a grapefruit, and more engaging to peel and eat.

Yet for all this farmland idyll, this was Israel and not Kansas. Bulldozers clearing out the foundations for a new neighborhood near my home unearthed an intact olive press probably dating back to the 2nd century BCE, with a jumble of massive carved stone weights still in place and a giant basalt grindstone lying on its side like a tractor tire in a garage. On walks through the forested hills at the edges of the village, we often encountered other telltale carvings in the soft limestone bedrock—shallow vats for pressing grapes— evidence of settlement during the early centuries of the Common

Era, or even earlier. Deeper carved stone steps leading down into the earth indicated entrances to ancient burial caves, now almost entirely filled in with soil and roots, convenient lairs for rabbits, porcupines and other wild animals.

The village of Beit Lehem Haglilit (Bethlehem of the Galilee, as distinguished from Bethlehem of Judea, outside of Jerusalem), just a brief hike up the hill from Alonei Aba, was mentioned by Joshua in the Book of Prophets as he delineated the territory allocated to the Tribe of Zebulon upon the Israelites' return from Egypt. Remains of both an ancient synagogue and a Byzantine church were discovered in this village, and I have been thrilled to find striated pot shards, opalescent chips of Roman glass and dice-like tesserae in its grassy fields.

On our outings, we frequently crossed paths with Bedouin men and women from neighboring villages, tending herds of sheep and goats, gleaning the harvested agricultural fields and gathering edible wild plants. For my husband, the Bedouins and their lifestyle were a natural and unremarkable part of the landscape. But I found it nothing short of miraculous to see how these age-old foodways were still being practiced in our times. And how much more natural and authentic these herders and gatherers seemed to me against the backdrop of ancient stones and fields than did the modern supermarket further up the road.

Our Bedouin neighbors were calling my attention to a style of local eating that connected directly and tangibly to the millennia-long history of this very land. Suddenly, it seemed entirely plausible that these 21st century shepherds were gathering the same edible plants and tending the same type of flocks as the treaders at the grape presses carved into these hills thousands of years ago. Here were threads that led straight back to nothing less than the archetypal underpinnings of Western civilization, and I was compelled to follow their trail.

Thus, I set out on an adventure, using the local foods of the Galilee as my compass, to trace the living links to the ancient past of my contemporary agricultural landscape. I spent hours at the Haifa University Library, reading up on Mediterranean food history. And inevitably, I found myself consulting the most articulate and venerable documentation available on how life was lived in this land during antiquity. For the first time since Sunday school, I went back to reading the Bible[1].

. . .

Many of the Bible's narratives play out across a landscape of herding and farming, where prosperity, deprivation, reward and retribution are all vividly expressed in agricultural metaphor. As I read, I marked every place where foods were mentioned, and my Bible soon sported a dense fringe of yellow Post-its. For my purposes, I decided to approach these references in their literal sense: as graphic depictions of what foods people ate in this region during ancient times and how they were procured. As I was to discover, much of what I was reading resonated deeply with my own experiences exploring the culinary landscape of the Galilee.

Living in the land of the scriptures made my appreciation of these ancient texts immeasurably more vivid. Yet it was my hard-earned fluency in Hebrew that enabled me to approach them in their original language, and to appreciate the nuance, ambiguity

---

[1]The Hebrew Bible, which includes the Five Books of Moses, the Prophets and the Writings.

and layers of meaning which were often lost in translation. What appeared simply as "grain" in English versions, for example, or even "corn" in some translations, could be described in the Hebrew text in as many terms as a baker has for bread.

At the same time, I began to investigate the culinary traditions as they are currently practiced in the various ethnic communities in the agricultural villages of the Galilee. I found people who are still pressing olive oil and grinding wheat under stones, and others who could recall when the only water they had was what was drawn from the village well. If this weren't remarkable enough, I also realized that, after thousands of years, many of these traditional practices and their living memory are most probably destined for extinction in our lifetime.

But as I looked around, no one seemed to be conscious of these historic developments. And no wonder, considering that these traditional foodways are being practiced, by and large, by Arab villagers. Even though they make up about half of the citizens of the Galilee, and one fifth of Israeli society overall, Israeli Arabs, whether they are Palestinian, Bedouin, Muslim, Christian, Druze, Circassian, or any combination thereof, may be the least familiar people in Israeli mainstream consciousness. Even among Israeli foodies, I found there was only the most cursory understanding of, or interest in traditional Arab foodways.

The reasons for this are very simple. In Israel today, Jewish and Arab societies exist with very little interaction between them. Precious few Israeli Arabs and Jews exchange hospitality in their homes. Thus, the average Jewish Israeli's experience of Arab food is limited to the formulaic fare of Middle Eastern restaurants, which presents about as faithful a reflection of its origins as that of American Chinese restaurants.

Traditional Arab home cooking is not found in restaurants. The kitchens of Arab restaurants are run by men, just as the kitchens at home are the domain of women. And Arab women, and their kitchens, are by and large protected from exposure to the outside world. Furthermore, as Liora Gvion notes in "Culinary Bridges versus Culinary Barriers," her important study of Palestinian cooking in Israel, keeping home cooking out of sight is one way Arab families have of withholding access to that cultural asset from Israeli Jewish society.

Yet in spite of all this, I found that, by exploring traditional foodways as they are practiced in Arab communities in the Galilee, an entire world opened up to me. With my interest in food extended as an olive branch, not only did I encounter hospitality instead of barriers, but I was invited time and again to sit down and break bread.

The discovery that food was such a powerful bridge across the Jewish-Arab divide was transformational. I found that, as much as I despaired over the seemingly intractable Israeli-Palestinian conflict and the painfully widespread discrimination against Israeli Arabs, on a personal level, the relationships I was developing with my Arab acquaintances through my interest in food were a source of profound happiness and optimism. Then I had a crazy thought: is it too naïve to believe that food could be a means for resolving the conflict between Jews and Arabs?

Of course I knew better.

Throughout history, dietary laws and customs have served

to unite and preserve Jewish peoplehood in a larger world. In this place and these times, however, I have chosen to approach food as a means of bringing people together instead of keeping them apart. If using food as a bridge between individuals from either side of the conflict can help overcome suspicion and promote mutual understanding, even on the most modest scale, then something very significant can be achieved. And what more could anyone hope for? It is in this spirit that I have written this book.

BEDOUINS

Edible Wild Plants

My Galilee Home

… the region of the Canaanites, the Hittites, the Amorites, the Perizzites, the Hivites, and the Jebustines. Exodus 3:8

In the Holy Land, names of places are layered one on top of the other like flaky coats of paint. Alonei Aba, the village I moved to and live in to this day, was previously christened Waldheim by German Christians, members of the Templer Society, who set down their stakes here in 1907 as part of a grand scheme to prepare the land for the Second Coming. The expanse of land on which they built their settlement, purchased from an absentee landowner living in Beirut, was known in Arabic as *Um el Amed*, perhaps referring to a massive old tree. The Templers also looked to the oak-covered hills when they chose the name "Waldheim," German for "forest home," for their new outpost in the land of the Bible.

Waldheim and the neighboring Beit Lehem of the Galilee were among a handful of agricultural villages established in Palestine by the Templers, along with urban communities in Tel Aviv, Jerusalem and Haifa. Strategically situated halfway between Haifa and Nazareth, the village of Waldheim was laid out like a cross, with a collection of formidable Bavarian-style stone farmhouses erected along its main streets and, in the center, a modest Romanesque-inspired stone church with a rooster weathervane topping its steeple. The Templers cultivated wheat and olives, grape vines and fruit trees in the land around the village, with the help of the local tenant farmers who had worked for the previous owner. Up the road, Beit Lehem was built by an ideologically distinct group of Templers, without a house of worship, atop the ancient ruins.

At that time, tribes of Bedouins were already setting up camps at the peripheries of Waldheim, Beit Lehem and the other agricultural settlements in this area, having migrated from Syria, Saudi Arabia and other neighboring lands over the previous century in pursuit of new pasture for their flocks. The Templers employed the Bedouins as watchmen to counter the age-old scourge of agricultural theft.

From the start, the Templers fared better under the Ottomans, whose centuries-long rule over the Holy Land was in its final days, than with the British, who assumed control over Mandatory Palestine after World War I. When the Second World War broke out, the Templers, supporters of the Third Reich, became enemies in their adopted land. The men of Waldheim were called up and back to Germany, while the women and children remained interned within the now fenced-off village, with British soldiers barracked inside. At the war's end, the remaining Templers were deported by the British, and with the fatherland in ruins, most of them settled in Australia.

During the same tumultuous post-war reshuffling, a few dozen Romanian Holocaust survivors, my future in-laws among them, boarded a ship bound for Palestine. They would reach their destination, however, only after a 12-month detour in a Cyprus internment camp, courtesy of the same agents of the British King. Their protracted journey ended in 1949 in the freshly-declared State of Israel, where the Jewish Agency checked the new immigrants for lice, issued ID cards, and packed them off to the abandoned houses of Waldheim. Like their predecessors, when it came to choosing a name for their new home, the Romanian newcomers drew inspiration from the surrounding forest, where "Alonei" in Hebrew is the plural possessive form of "oaks." "Aba" commemorated the fallen paratrooper, Aba Berdicev, their comrade from Romania.

The refugees-turned-pioneers set aside memories of the horrors left behind and immersed themselves in creating the institutions of a cooperative kibbutz settlement, replete with wrenching agricultural labor and the paradigm-shifting task of replacing German, Romanian and Yiddish mother-tongues with Hebrew. Many of the neighboring Bedouins continued to work the land alongside the new Jewish settlers, as they had done with the Germans, and do so to this day.

By the time I arrived here in the late 1980's, Alonei Aba's kibbutz lifestyle had long since been abandoned in favor of a less constrictive cooperative framework, and the Bedouins of the Galilee had traded their nomadic lifestyle for settled village living. The expanse of oak forest had been declared a nature reserve, and strung in a constellation around it were the Bedouin villages of Hilf-Tabash, Bosmat Tabun, Kaabiye, and Hajajra, on one side, and the Jewish communities of Beit Lehem, Alonei Aba and Kibbutz Alonim on the other. Ron had many friends in the Bedouin villages and we often visited them for coffee or meals in their homes.

My first encounters with Bedouin hospitality were in the home of Abdallah and Fatma from Kaabiye. Abdallah worked with Ron in the dairy, and at that time he was already close to retirement. He had known my husband since Ron was a child, and both Abdallah and his wife loved him like a son. Beanstalk thin and slightly stooped, Abdallah was never without a white *keffiye* draped like a lopsided turban on his head and a toothy smile that would light up his eyes and send his cheekbones skyward. Every day he would cross the nature reserve on an ancient, faded cherry-red Ferguson tractor that puttered along at a comic-strip pace. Abdallah and Ron would meet at 4 in the morning in the milking parlor, and, at the end of their shift, share a breakfast that Fatma had prepared of fresh pita bread, mashed potatoes seasoned with olive oil, home-made yoghurt known as *leben*, and Fatma's olives.

Some afternoons, after work and the rest hour that followed it, we would make our way to Abdallah and Fatma's home. In those early visits, we lounged on mattresses on the floor of the main salon, while the men chatted about work and family and I tried to catch a word of Hebrew here and there. In the center of the room stood a polished brass brazier on low legs, with hot coals that Abdallah would tend with a set of tongs. Nestled among the coals were four or five polished brass coffee pots with spouts as grand as a toucan's beak. From one of those pots, he would pour into a single cup a sip of the intense, sour, long-brewed black coffee called *saada* for each of us in turn—the refreshment of hospitality that is extended in welcome to every honored guest.

If we were fortunate enough to stay for dinner, the meal was served on an expansive stainless steel tray, carried out from the interior of the house and set down on the floor. Arranged in splashes of color on the tray, depending on the season, were mounds of summer-ripe tomato and cucumber salad, home-cured cracked green olives, snowy *labaneh*—a smooth, sour cheese made from the milk of a neighbor's sheep, rich reddish-brown *mejadra* made of bulgur wheat and tiny dark lentils, drawing its color from patiently-stewed onions; and a bowl of *malukhiye*—a gelatinous vivid green soup made of the leaves of the jute plant. Together with Abdallah, Fatma and whichever of their ten daughters happened to be home at the time, we knelt on the floor around this bounty, dipping pieces of pita bread into the different dishes, and enjoying the easy conviviality of eating knee to knee and eye to eye.

• • •

Abel became a keeper of sheep, and Cain became a tiller of the soil.
Genesis 4:2

For me, these glimpses into Bedouin society simply added to the fascination of my Galilee home. With my urban American background, living among people of different ethnic backgrounds felt comfortable and right. As fortune would have it, landing in the Galilee had placed me in Israel's most ethnically and culturally diverse region, where about half of the 1.8 million residents are Arab. Yet behind this opaque, monolithic statistic, I was to discover an intricate and complex demography.

There are dozens of Arab villages, towns and cities all across the Galilee, and it has taken me time to appreciate the complexities of culture and identity within them. While the villages near my own home are predominantly Bedouin, many others are populated by *fellaheen*—the traditional subsistence farmers of this land—and their descendents. Thousands of years after Cain and Abel, traces of this ancient dichotomy of farmer and herder still inform local Arab society, even as the actual practice of these livelihoods has largely been abandoned.

There are Druze villages scattered across the Galilee and the Golan Heights. Their religion has its origins in Zoroastrianism; its rituals are the guarded secret of the observant, and marriage outside of it is forbidden. Cities like Nazareth and its smaller neighbor Shefar'am once had significant Christian populations, now replaced by Muslim majorities; of the few predominantly Christian villages that remain, most are in the Western Galilee, near the Lebanese border. In a number of communities, like the town of Mghrar, Druze, Muslim and Christian residents live as neighbors. And in two small Galilee villages, the Circassians of Israel fiercely preserve their language and cultural identity, both of which can be traced back to the Caucasus, before they were driven out of their homeland in the 19th century by the Russians and repatriated as warriors throughout the Ottoman Empire.

The trajectories that Jewish and Arab communities of the Galilee have followed to reach the present day are radically skewed. In 1948, the Jewish citizens of the freshly-established State of Israel, many of whom emigrated from industrially advanced Europe, were intently at work building the new nation, creating modern cities, villages and cooperative settlements based on advanced commercial scale agriculture. At the same time, their Arab neighbors, whether urbanites, *fellaheen* or Bedouins, were seeing their known world—one which in many ways differed little from that described in the ancient texts—coming to an end. With only limited participation in the astounding progress that defines modern Israel, the Arabs of the

Galilee had no choice but to shift, as one historian described, from first to fourth gear, in a society that often only begrudgingly made room for them.

Israeli Jews and Arabs tend to orient themselves to a physical world that is charted out on two separate maps, superimposed one on top of the other, with few common landmarks. Exploring traditional foodways in the Galilee presented me with a unique opportunity to traverse the two worlds. A Jewish woman with American-accented Hebrew, I approached men and women from different cultures with courtesy and a sincere interest in learning about their culinary traditions. In return, gatherers, farmers and cooks of every ethnic background graciously shared their knowledge and invited me into their homes and hearts.

The Brothers Saadi

Every journey unfolds under a unique constellation of circumstances. On this particular January afternoon I was almost fifty years
old, living in a rural village in the Lower Galilee, and married to a
dairy farmer who had left the cow shed over a decade earlier to join
the police force. My work as a freelance writer was finished for the
day. Lunch had been prepared and served to my two sons after they
had come home from school, and the dishes were washed. The boys,
comfortably engrossed in their television program, were finally old
enough to be left home alone. Outdoors, a light breeze, azure sky
and mercifully warm sun enticed me out for a walk in the fields.

Only a few steps from my front door, I turned off onto a dirt
road leading down to the fields. This was a Galilee winter day at its
finest—when the cool air is an elixir, the green wheat fields sway
and glow in the breeze, and the sun, so brutal during the rest of the
year, can actually be greeted face to face. On each side of the path,
Queen Anne's lace the size of dinner plates reached as high as my
shoulders, bringing back memories of East Coast summers.

Down the path, a figure was making its way up the hill towards
me—an older man, walking alone, carrying a small plastic bag. As

the distance between us lessened, I saw that he was from one of the Bedouin villages, taking advantage of this brilliant day to collect edible wild plants. We might easily have passed each other, perhaps nodding hello, and simply continued along our separate ways. But for years I'd wanted to know more about the Bedouins and their edible wild plants, and on that particular day, curiosity and courage trumped timidity and awkwardness with my adopted language. In a momentary burst of inspiration, I offered up the Arabic greeting, *Salam Aleikum*, then switched to my heavily accented Hebrew.

"What are you picking?" I asked. After a moment's hesitation, the gentleman surrendered to the imperative of courtesy and stopped to reply. He was tall and trim, in neatly-pressed work clothes, and his balding head was shiny as a chestnut. Reaching into the bag he was holding, he pulled out a cluster of deep green, diamond-shaped leaves. "This is *selek*," he explained. "My wife makes *ftayir* with it. She washes the leaves, chops them, then crushes them with salt to make a filling. That goes into dough, and then you have *ftayir*."

Seeing that I was genuinely interested in what he was saying, he warmed up. "These wild plants are the healthiest food you can eat," he told me emphatically.

"And I want to learn all about them," I exclaimed, swept up in his enthusiasm.

"Well, if you really want to learn", he said magnanimously, "I can teach you. I know all about these plants. My name is M. Saadi— you can find me in Bosmat Tabun." Then we went our separate ways.

Thrilled with my new project, I recruited Ron to help me find M. Saadi. A few days later we drove across the nature reserve to the minimarket in Bosmat Tabun. Ron asked the proprietor if he could direct us to M. Saadi's house. In Bosmat Tabun, as in any small village, everyone tends to know everyone else. "M. Saadi?" he laughed. "There must be a dozen M. Saadis here." In Bosmat Tabun there are two clans—the Saadis and the Z'beidats—and the Saadi clan is about three times larger. Finally, mustering every detail I could remember, we narrowed down our search and found ourselves at the door of a small orderly home, with flower pots outside on the cement courtyard.

M. himself answered the door, clearly shocked to see me, turning up like a bad penny. But he recovered his composure and invited us inside. He sent his grown daughter, just as unnerved by this unexpected company as he was, to prepare coffee. "I want to learn about edible wild plants," I explained again. "Are you still willing to teach me?" He excused himself and we could hear him and his daughter in the kitchen angrily exchanging words. Then he returned to the living room and explained that it would be impossible.

We quickly finished our coffee and headed home. I was mortified to have my earnest effort so summarily rebuffed, and pondered what to do next. But then Ron had an idea. After years of dealing with agricultural theft, he had, coincidentally, come to know M. Saadi's brother Salim, who worked as a watchman in a nearby avocado grove. He would talk to Salim, he promised. Maybe he would be willing to meet with me.

•   •   •

A few days later, Ron took me to meet Salim Saadi in the avocado orchard of Kibbutz Alonim. It was another exceptionally beautiful winter day, and that morning we found Salim sitting under a giant oak tree in the leafy serenity of the orchard. Salim was shorter and older than his brother, dressed for work in knee-high rubber boots and a knit stocking cap. He also had a softer manner, and, out of friendship, was gracious about showing Ron's foreign wife the basics of edible wild plants.

Literally at our feet, Salim started our lesson. "This is *ellet*" (wild chicory), he explained, picking a starburst of long, thin, scalloped leaves. "It is good for cleaning the blood. You chop it fine, cook it in boiling water, and then squeeze out all the liquid. After that, the greens are cooked with onion in a little olive oil. But you can also eat it raw, just as it is, with bread." Each of us bit off a piece of *ellet* leaf, and the bitterness, which for me was overwhelming, he clearly savored.

Luf is a dark green fleshy leaf that I'd often seen growing in my yard, but with its baroque curves and ominous, toxic-looking shine, I never imagined it could be edible. Salim showed me how to fold the leaf in half and carefully tear away the stem and fibrous central rib. "*Luf* has to be specially prepared before it can be eaten. Most animals stay away from *luf*—it's only eaten by people and porcupines."

The ubiquitous, frilly-leaved *hubeisa* (mallow) is probably the most common edible wild plant in the fields. High in iron, Salim explained, it too can be chopped and fried with onion. "*Hubeisa* is good for people with diabetes and cholesterol."

Next he proffered a tough-stemmed tall leafy plant that looked like celery in thorns. "This is *salawiya*—you can eat it raw." I bit into the stem, and the horseradish intensity of the fleshy fibers took my breath away. Salim smiled. "That sharpness is the best thing for opening up your appetite."

We found a patch of wild cyclamens in a small grove of oaks

bordering the orchard, and Salim picked one of its heart-shaped leaves, which just about filled the palm of his hand. Then he rolled it between his fingers, showing how these leaves can be filled with rice and cooked like stuffed grape leaves. He then moved on to *el-saina*, a member of the sage family, whose large, bumpy-textured leaves look like the tongues after which they are named, and can also be filled and prepared the same way.

Nearby, out of a cloud of thorny brush, Salim picked a single tall stalk of wild asparagus. "This is *hilayon*—good for the kidneys. Eating it cleans out your whole system." Salim recommended cooking it the Bedouin way, with eggs. "We Bedouins would rather eat these greens than lamb."

After we finished our tour of the orchard, we sat down to rest under the giant oak. Salim told me about how, as a young man, he'd worked as a tracker for the Israeli police. Like many Bedouins, he was exceptionally in tune with the ground under his feet, and his ability to detect footprints made him a valuable team member— particularly in cases of terrorist infiltration. His tracking skills, he told me proudly, helped solve the case of the Scorpion Pass terrorist attack in 1954. Many years later, during a short hospitalization, the man in the bed next to him, an American writer, was so impressed with his stories that he wrote a book about him, called "The Scout". "It is in English", he explained apologetically. But he promised to give me a copy anyway.

Now, as a pensioner, Salim comes to the avocado orchard every day during the season to guard over the trees laden with fruit. I asked him if his children also gather wild plants. "One of my sons is a doctor, one is a medical technician, one is a member of the bus company cooperative, and my daughter is a teacher," he replied, as if this was explanation enough. I asked him how long the young Bedouins would continue to carry on this tradition of winter gathering. His face twisted with the scorn of a person of years sizing up the younger generation in the direst fashion. "Too many of the young ones don't have any respect for the old traditions—they smoke hashish and the girls refuse to get married."

Ellet-Chicory Salad

They shall eat the flesh that same night; they shall eat it roasted over the fire, with unleavened bread and with bitter herbs. Exodus 12:8

Bitter herbs are generally associated with the Passover seder ritual, where they serve as a reminder of the bitterness of exile. In the lexicon of edible wild plants, bitterness is considered to be healthful and invigorating. The Galilee's springtime wild growth offers numerous edible plants that fit the bitter bill. The all time favorite in these parts, however, is chicory.

- 1 bunch chicory, cleaned and chopped into smaller than bite-sized pieces (endive can be substituted)

- 1 small onion, thinly sliced

- 2 Tbsp ground sumac

- Olive oil, plenty of lemon juice and salt to taste

Combine all ingredients in a bowl and toss well.

Picking *Hubeisa* with Nadia

Can what is tasteless be eaten without salt?
Does mallow juice have any flavor? Job 6:6

Hubeisa (mallow) comes from the Arabic word *hubs* meaning bread, and its edible patty-like buds, when peeled, actually look like little pita breads. But it is the leaves and stems that are the plant's main source of sustenance. *Hubeisa* is, in fact, the staff of foraging life. When Jerusalem was under siege during Israel's War of Independence, the city's residents famously subsisted on *hubeisa*. For many Israelis, this anecdote encapsulates their only knowledge of this ubiquitous local edible wild plant.

Hubeisa grows everywhere—in the grittiest city lots, by roadsides and in open fields. But the best *hubeisa* for eating—with stalks smooth of stiff hairs, growing in a clean area that hasn't been sprayed or exposed to exhaust fumes—is more difficult to find. Nadia from Kaabiye has graciously introduced me to several of her favorite *hubeisa* picking spots. A single woman in her 30s, Nadia cleans homes in Alonei Aba and Beit Lehem; her father, Ahmed, worked side by side with my father-in-law in the orchards of Alonei Aba, and her brother milked in the dairy at various times with my husband and

---

both of my sons. Their family numbers among the few in Kaabiye who still keep a herd of sheep and goats; Ahmed takes them out to graze in the hills on fine days, and Bahiya, Nadia's mother, is in charge of the milking and the production of *leben* and *labaneh*.

Nadia loves to be outdoors in the fresh air, picking. She has often told me that during the season there is nowhere else she'd rather be. It was Nadia who taught me how to run my fingers over the *hubeisa* stalks to find the smoothest ones to pick. Bent over with our bags and plastic-handled kitchen knives, we have waded side by side through knee-high seas of wild mallow. Nadia picks twice as fast as I do, assembling fat bouquets, and then deftly tying each one into a neat bundle using a long *hubeisa* stalk.

Nadia's mother has a taste for *hubeisa* which must be satisfied. On fine winter days, Nadia will drive her mother and a back-seat full of grandchildren to their favorite picking fields. Bahiya is old and stout and has painfully swollen legs, but she will not give up these outings. One day I arranged to meet Nadia and her mother to pick *hubeisa* and cook outdoors. I would bring a portable gas burner, we agreed, and she would bring the pot.

We met in a huge open field on the outskirts of Beit Lehem, which, once you knew what to look for, looked less like a mass of weeds and more like a giant greengrocer. In no time we had collected a large pile of the smooth-stalked greens.

Bahiya, wrapped in layers of scarves and an apron, sat herself down in the field to cook. The flame from the gas burner wasn't hot enough to suit her, so with sticks, leaves and an old plank that Nadia scavenged, she quickly lit a small, crackling fire. On a low-legged wooden cutting board they'd brought from home, she chopped a few onions and tossed them into the battered aluminum pot where they were soon browning in a generous pool of oil. Then she set to work on the *hubeisa*, chopping it over and over until it was a crumbly green pile which she tossed into the pot with a fistful of salt. Like the mother of us all, Bahiya sat with her legs splayed in front of her fire, fanning the flame with the hem of her dress—in high spirits to be cooking outdoors, just like old times.

I asked her if she thought women were better off today than when she was young. "We used to work hard," she said, "but you didn't have to clean so much—the tent didn't have a floor or windows that needed to be washed. But today, we have everything, and if a woman were suddenly left without electricity or water, she would starve."

Zaatar

Take a bunch of hyssop, dip it in the blood that is in the basin,
and apply some of the blood that is in the basin to the lintel and
to the two doorposts. Exodus 12:22

Purge me with hyssop till I am pure. Psalm 51:9

Of all the wild herbs native to the Galilee, the humble *zaatar* plant is undoubtedly the most popular. *Zaatar*, or specifically the namesake spice mixture in which this indigenous herb stars, is the salt and pepper of seasonings in almost every Arab home, and many others as well.

In the Bible, *zaatar*, referred to by its Hebrew name, *ezov*, is described as a ritual purifier, used in combination with cedar wood and "crimson stuff" (or a "crimson worm," depending on the translation) to purify the home of a leper, or anyone defiled by a corpse. In the final episode of the "ten plagues" narrative, the Israelites are instructed to dip branches of *ezov* into the blood of a sacrificed lamb, then mark their doorposts as a sign that the house should be "passed over" by the avenging Lord (the prototype of the mezuzah placed at the entrance to Jewish homes.) In Psalm 51:9, King David

21

calls for *ezov* to ease his troubled conscience after his desire for the beautiful Batsheva led him to send her husband, Uriah the Hittite, to certain death in the battlefield.

In English, *zaatar* is commonly referred to as hyssop—a misnomer which traces back to the translation of the Hebrew Bible into Greek, when *ezov* became *hyssopus*. In our times, here in the Galilee, the plant's Latin name is *origanum syriacum*, although in English, it is called Syrian marjoram. I think I'll just call it *zaatar*.

> *He discoursed about trees, from the cedar in Lebanon to the*
> *hyssop that grows out of the wall…* I Kings 5:13

Zaatar grows wild in the forested hills of the Galilee—a modest, low-growing plant with small round, fleshy leaves steeped in potent essential oils. Sometimes, I'll see *zaatar* growing out of a crack in a limestone boulder. The leaves of the *zaatar* plant, dried and ground, then blended with sesame seeds, ground sumac and olive oil, are the basic components of the local *zaatar* seasoning mixture.

The *zaatar* spice mixture appears in different forms in Lebanon, Syria and other Middle Eastern countries. One *zaatar* recipe I found from Turkey lists thyme, chickpeas and watermelon seeds in the ingredients. The plant that provides the foundation for *zaatar* mixtures also differs according to region, and basically refers to that member of the *Labiatae* family which grows on the local hillside, whether it is a variety of thyme, marjoram, oregano or savory.

For local Arab families, *manakish*, fresh pita bread baked with a topping of *zaatar* mixture moistened with olive oil, is a standard breakfast food. It is served to schoolchildren in the belief that the *zaatar* will sharpen their minds, particularly before a big test.

Zaatar is also frequently sprinkled on *labaneh*, and with fresh pita becomes another breakfast staple.

But *zaatar* can also be eaten fresh. I love *zaatar* salad, which is simply fresh *zaatar* leaves mixed with finely chopped lemon, and onion, dressed with olive oil, lemon juice and sumac. The pungent, appetite-inducing quality of the *zaatar* leaves is a reminder that it belongs to the same family of plants as mint and oregano.

The Galilee Society, a research institute in Shefar'am that focuses on Arab traditional medicine in Israel and the West Bank, conducted a survey among practitioners of traditional medicine, to identify the local plants they used in their treatments. The survey, which was published in the *Journal of Ethnopharmacology*, lists 129 local plants. Among them, *zaatar* was reported as being used to treat disorders ranging from diabetes to skin conditions to liver, respiratory and gastrointestinal ailments. An infusion of one teaspoon of *zaatar* leaves in one cup of boiling water is described as a remedy for intestinal pain, inflammation and high blood pressure. As a tea or infused in olive oil, *zaatar* has traditionally been used to treat headaches, coughs, earaches, intestinal parasites and eczema; to strengthen the heart; to soothe toothaches and gum disease; and to strengthen and whiten teeth.

At the Neve Yaar Agricultural Research Center, not far from the Alonei Aba Nature Reserve, Dr. Nativ Dudai is studying the unique characteristics of the *zaatar* plant, and how they can be enhanced in newly bred varieties. *Zaatar*, he explains, contains high concentrations of thymol, carvacrol and other phenols which exert anti-bacterial, anti-oxidant, fungicidal, insecticidal and nematicidal effects. As an anti-spasmodic, it eases painful peristaltic muscular contractions. It even works as an analgesic, so that if a person with a toothache chews on a few *zaatar* leaves, it will not only treat the infected area, but also relieve the pain.

But one of the more original uses for *zaatar* I heard from our friend Mahmoud, who told me that shepherds coming home in the evening used to rub their hands and necks with *zaatar* leaves so they would greet their wives with a fragrant smell.

. . .

In 1978, the Israeli Nature Reserves Authority initiated a law that granted *zaatar* protected status and mandated substantial fines for anyone caught picking it for commercial use. Salman Abu Rukun, now Head of External Relations at the renamed Israel Nature and Parks Authority, was a warden at the time, and was involved in creating the new legislation. He remembers observing caravans of pick-up trucks leaving the nature reserves day after day loaded with sacks full of *zaatar*. A contractor would arrive at the park in the morning and drop off a group of women with empty sacks, returning in the evening to pick them up with their cash crop. When questioned, they told him that the *zaatar* was destined for markets in Kuwait, Oman and Saudi Arabia, via Jordan. Concerned that over-picking would decimate the plant stock, the Parks Authority took steps to have it protected. "*Zaatar* is one of the very few plants that flowers in the summer, so it is a critical source of sustenance for the bees," Abu Rukun explained. "The absence of *zaatar* in this fragile eco-system would have disastrous consequences."

With no guidelines for what comprised "commercial use," however, the Parks Authority wardens found the new ruling difficult to enforce. For many local Arab families, *zaatar* picking was an integral part of a springtime picnic ritual, when the leaves are still large and plump from the winter rain. While some members of the family went off to search for *zaatar*, the others laid out the picnic lunch. Then, after eating, the women and children set to work pulling the leaves off the stems. If everyone was efficient, they would come home with enough to last the family for an entire year, until the next picking season. How does one prove to a park warden that this quantity is for personal consumption only?

In 1998, the law was amended to prohibit the picking of *zaatar* under any circumstances. Abu Rukun was not consulted about this new legislation, and if he had known beforehand, he admits, he would have tried to prevent it. "I objected, and the whole thing is hard for me—I know that you can love nature through the stomach."

The Parks Authority conducted an extensive education campaign in the Arab sector, which included broadcasting radio and television messages and distributing cultivated *zaatar* seedlings for planting in home gardens. Abu Rukun hopes that enforcement and education, together with home cultivation, will enable wild zaatar to replenish, and the protected status can one day be repealed. In the meantime, the economics of *zaatar* consumption are clear—either one picks it out in nature at the risk of receiving an extremely stiff fine, grows one's own, or buys cultivated *zaatar*, fresh, dried, or ready-mixed.

Tony Kanaza, owner of the El Babour Galilee Mill in Nazareth, a 100-year-old former wheat mill-turned spice emporium and Galilee institution, purchases cultivated *zaatar* from local growers and produces a *zaatar* mixture according to the store's own special blend. "Women are busy working and don't have time to go out and pick anymore," he explains, politely side-stepping the protected plant issue and the fact that Arab women are among the most under-employed sectors of the Israeli population.

As we sat in Tony's office under the vaulted ceilings of El Babour, a distinguished elderly gentleman in long robes and a white *keffiye*, sitting in the corner quietly puffing on a cigarette, commented on how *zaatar* had gone from being the food for people who had nothing to a precious commodity. In fact, for almost as long as people have been living on this land, a piece of bread, olive oil and a little *zaatar* have comprised the basic diet of subsistence.

The *Mukhtar*

The one person I knew who would be able to paint a vivid picture of Bedouin foodways before the changes of the last few decades was Mustafa Tabash, the *Mukhtar*, or tribal head, of Hilf-Tabash. A small man in his seventies, with an outsized presence and piercing black eyes, Mustafa is a fountain of information on Bedouin culture and a famous story-teller with a wicked sense of humor. He and Ron's father were close friends over decades, and the affection with which he greets my husband always touches me.

One afternoon, we visited Mustafa in the smaller of the two tents he kept outside his home in which to receive guests. As we sat on low stools around a radiant wood stove, Mustafa started off by explaining his family's lineage in the tribal hierarchy. The position of *Mukhtar* of a Bedouin tribe, he explained, was once an official appointment—a respected individual chosen to serve as the mediator between the members of a tribe and the government authorities. Coming from a long line of tribal leaders, Mustafa's grandfather was a tribal judge under the Ottoman government, and his father was appointed *Mukhtar* by the British Mandate authority that followed. He himself received his appointment from the Israeli

Ministry of the Interior in 1960. Officially, the role of *Mukhtar* has now been replaced by the head of the local community council—an elected position which Mustafa's son held until recently—but, as *Mukhtar*, Mustafa was still a figure of authority, busy mediating tribal issues beyond the scope of government institutions, such as brokering *sulkha*s (peace treaties) to resolve conflicts between individuals and tribes.

I asked Mustafa about the winter wild plant gathering among the Bedouins, and how it has changed over time. Mustafa tucked in the edge of his white *keffiye* as he spoke. "In the old days, the Bedouins had no money, and no need for it—we lived in tents, without water or electricity. In the summer we raised tomatoes, cucumbers and melons, and in the winter, we ate the plants and mushrooms we collected in the fields. We also grew chickpeas, lentils and wheat, from which we made flour, bulgur and *freekeh* (roasted green wheat). We collected bee hives in the forest and made special honey out of carob pods. The herd provided milk for making *leben* and *labaneh* and meat for special occasions. Once a year we'd sell a lamb or two and with the money, buy coffee and sugar."

"Today, when I suggest that one of my daughters collect *hubeisa*, or milk the goat, she'll look at her soft, clean hands and start making excuses. She would rather buy things at the store. But when she gets a taste for real *labaneh*, she sends one of her children over to our house to ask her mother for 'just a little bit.' But if she wants just a little, then why does she send such a big bowl?"

Labaneh

Pour 2 cups of yoghurt (at least 4.5% fat) into a cheesecloth bag. Suspend overnight to let the water drain out. The next day, collect the cheese from the cloth and put it in a bowl. Spread on a dish, top with olive oil, *zaatar* mixture or even a sprinkling of fresh *zaatar* leaves, and serve with fresh pita for dipping.

Cooking *Luf* with Hal'la

Cooking *luf* has been my consummate challenge. At first it was hard for me to believe that this plant is edible, so sinister looking are its extravagant, waxy leaves. In fact, *luf* bears a potent toxin that keeps most nibblers at bay, and which must be neutralized in the cooking process. I would have dismissed *luf* entirely, except that every Bedouin I ever met has spoken so ardently about its delicate flavor and extraordinarily healthful properties that I knew I had to at least try it.

Luf grows in profusion in my very own yard, so one day I picked a pile of leaves and set about preparing them. I removed the stem and spine, per Nadia's instructions, then finely chopped the leaves and sautéed them in olive oil with onion, adding a generous portion of lemon juice. The first forkful was indeed delicious, but after the second, I started to feel an intense prickling in the roof of my mouth, in my tongue and in my throat, which was decidedly uncomfortable. Trying not to panic, I sucked on a piece of lemon, remembering that this was supposed to be the neutralizing agent, and after some minutes the toxic effect subsided. When I related the experience to Nadia, she found it quite amusing, but I knew it would be a long time before I could contemplate cooking *luf* again.

The following year, however, the new growth of *luf* plants appeared in my yard like a tossed gauntlet and it was clear I would have to prepare it again. This time I vowed to do it correctly. The opportunity presented itself one day when Ron and I were in Kaabiye visiting Fatma and Abdallah. That day, their grown daughter Hal'la happened to be visiting her parents.

Over coffee, I explained my interest in *luf* to Fatma and Hal'la. As always, my knowledge of, and interest in gathering edible wild plants gave us a pleasant topic for conversation. Fatma speaks very little Hebrew but Hal'la was able to translate for us. There's nothing to cooking *luf*, Hal'la assured me. She invited me to visit her in the nearby village of Ayadat so she could teach me how to prepare it.

A few days later I filled one large plastic bag with *luf* collected in and around my yard, and another with lemons, and made the twenty-minute drive to Hal'la's home. Hal'la is a warm and gracious woman in her late 20s—a housewife and mother of five. Her jovial husband, Ayeda, teaches Hebrew in the local Arab high school.

We sat at the dining room table of her neat and well-appointed home and sorted the leaves, removing the tough stem and spine of each leaf, then folding it in half and placing it on a pile. About half of the leaves I'd picked—the young, tender-looking ones—ended up in the reject pile with the stems. They were, as Hal'la translated from Arabic, "brother of *luf*"—actually calla leaves—and would ruin the dish.

With the spine-removing operation finished, Hal'la showed me how to take a pile of the folded leaves, wrap a large leaf around them, and slice the whole roll in half. She then put one rolled half on top of the other and cut through them, producing a pile of thin, deep green chiffonade. When that was done, we chopped onions, sautéed them in plenty of olive oil, and when they were transparent, added the shredded *luf*. Soon the *luf* was giving off plenty of liquid and Hal'la kept stirring the mixture so it would steam away. This, she assured me, would prevent any unpleasant sensation in one's mouth.

When most of the liquid had evaporated, she added a full cup of water and again stirred constantly until that, too, disappeared. I squeezed juice from half a dozen lemons and we added it to the mixture—after about an hour of cooking, the *luf* was a deep green, thick stew, and ready to eat.

While we were cooking, Ayeda had gone out to buy fresh pita bread, from which we broke off bite-sized pieces, and we dug in with gusto. Yes, it did have a very earthy, distinctive flavor. But within seconds I felt a mild tingling on the roof of my mouth, this time not intense enough to prevent me from sharing in the pleasure of the meal. Could it be that *luf* and I were not meant to be? I brought home a plate of *luf* and offered it to Ron. He enjoyed it thoroughly, with no notable side effects.

The Sisters From Bosmat Tabun

Ron and I were returning from a long winter walk when we first encountered Maryam, her sister-in-law and her daughter-in-law in an empty field in the moshav, filling their plastic bags with great armloads of shiny green *selek* leaves. With a smile, I approached the women and asked about their gathering. They were clearly relieved that I wasn't coming to accuse them of trespassing.

Maryam, a stocky woman in her early 50s, answered first. She showed me the *selek* leaves which, at this point, I already knew how to identify. "Are you going to make *ftayir* with them?" I asked. Amazed that I was familiar with this traditional Arab dish, she became even more animated. "Where are you from?" she asked. "I can tell by your accent you're not from here." I told her that I was from the United States and the three women started to giggle. "Do you know Ridge? From *The Bold and the Beautiful?*" they asked. "We love that show", the daughter-in-law explained, a cheerful young woman in her twenties who was dressed in jeans and a sweater with her tied-back hair uncovered. "And do you know why? Because they do everything we aren't allowed to do."

Now it was my turn to ask where they were from. Bosmat

Tabun they replied. I told them that I was learning about edible wild plants and about my lesson with Salim. "Why don't you come to my home and cook with us?" Maryam offered. "We can show you how to make *ftayir*." I took her number, with a feeling that my next visit to Bosmat Tabun would be more auspicious.

It took a few weeks, but one late afternoon, I made the five-minute drive to the Bedouin village across the nature reserve. Like almost every Arab village I've ever visited, there are no street signs or house numbers, so I navigated according to Maryam's directions, following the main street, past the vegetable stores and the mosque, its dome and minaret newly gilded in gold leaf. From this mosque, the muezzin's call to prayer reaches Alonei Aba five times a day, and at 4 a.m., wafts into my bedroom window and weaves itself into my dreams. Together with my visit to M. Saadi, this was only the second time I'd ventured into the heart of Bosmat Tabun.

I found the house, and knocked on the door with one hand, a plate of freshly-baked chocolate chip cookies in the other. Maryam welcomed me into the small narrow family room. Her younger sister Emna and their school-aged daughters were all seated on long mattresses on the floor, next to a low wood stove, and they made room for me to join them. On the walls were pictures of the Al Aksa Mosque in Jerusalem, and framed quotes from the Koran. Maryam had already prepared dough, tweaked with dried, crushed anise seeds, several hours earlier. The filling for the *ftayir*, finely chopped *selek* and *zaatar* seasoned with plenty of lemon juice, salt and hot red pepper sauce, was heaped in a large plastic bowl.

Maryam pulled off fat handfuls of billowy dough and, on a wooden work surface mounted on low legs, we took turns kneading them into balls. After rolling each ball flat, Emna cut out circles of dough with the lid of an electric kettle, and I topped them with brimming tablespoons of the shiny green filling. The women showed me how to fold the edges of the dough around the filling to form a triangle, then, with practiced hands, pinched them together. My dough pinching somehow didn't manage to keep the *ftayir* from splitting at the seams, and Emna discreetly re-sealed them. The daughters took turns piercing the finished pastries with a fork, and Maryam carried them, tray by tray, to the small kitchen, then into the oven.

Emna, sharp and inquisitive, was a clear contrast to her heavy and world-weary older sister. She asked me about my children, my husband and my family, and then told me about her own. She and her sister had married brothers, and now they live next door to one another, drifting casually between one house and the other. When they were newly married, both Maryam and Emna worked at a Jewish-owned textile factory and it was there that they acquired basic conversational Hebrew. The mother tongue of none of us, it was still our only language in common. As we sat working the dough, the conversation frequently switched back to Arabic, and despairing at the prospect of ever learning such a daunting language, I resigned myself to letting the women's genial voices cascade over me.

The *ftayir* emerged from the oven brown and shiny, festive in their polka-dot piercing. Biting into the crusty dough released a steamy burst of anise, followed by moist, earthy sourness, and finally a burning bite of hot pepper. Absolutely addicting. Suddenly the living room was full of neighbors and relatives, all munching on the fresh *ftayir*—emptying each platter as it emerged from the kitchen. The plate on which I had brought the cookies was stacked high with steaming brown triangles for me to take home.

Baking *ftayir* with Maryam and Emna has become an annual tradition, although sometimes, off-season, I'll come just for a visit, to either one of their homes. We discuss our children and where we grocery shop, our exercise regimens and their constant struggle to lose weight. The novelty of having a Jewish woman in their homes has almost worn off, and their children are less bashful when I am around.

In a small but poignant gesture of intimacy, the sisters will pull back their head coverings and expose their hair, and we comment on how all of us are graying—a bittersweet moment of middle-aged solidarity. They seem to be much less comfortable visiting in my home, where the cats roam freely inside, and everything from the size of the glasses I serve drinks in to the coffee I prepare seems strange to them. But I invite them nonetheless.

Wild Asparagus

After seemingly endless, smoldering, dusty-brown days of autumn, the lush green of winter is exhilarating. Gathering edible wild plants, I find, is the perfect way to revel in the season. The time for gathering begins around late December, when the winter rains have worked their magic and the summer-parched land returns to life. And it comes to an end around Passover, when the first days of intense heat draw the snakes out of hibernation and they sun themselves, unseen, in the tall undergrowth, perilous landmines for the unwitting forager. All year long, I anxiously wait for these few precious months.

Beyond the visual delights of the winter wildflowers' gorgeous display, gathering edible wild plants gives me a mission, and focuses my attention on the shapes, colors and settings of the various green leaves. When I find a beautiful *selek* plant, or a large, handsomely shaped *elsaina* leaf, I'm as thrilled as a treasure hunter, and the regret of taking each leaf out of its natural setting is alleviated by the knowledge that two may grow back in its place.

Then there is the cooking. Preparing *hubeisa* or *selek* is not like opening a bag of greens from the supermarket. The leaves have to be sorted, trimmed, washed carefully and chopped, a time-consuming process that I have patiently come to terms with, because the reward is in the results. There is nothing more satisfying than a flavorful, healthy meal of mallow, wild spinach or wild asparagus that, only a few hours earlier, was drawing its energies from the earth of the surrounding hillsides. It is the perfect culmination of a Galilee winter day.

I learned from Shimi, a passionate advocate and practitioner of a more contemporary, new-age approach to local eating, that there are three rules to foraging. The first, and my favorite, is that one should only eat what tastes good. This will usually prevent inadvertent poisoning, and may even ensure that what you are consuming is exactly what your body is asking for. The second rule relates to the flow of energy—that the forager should eat the parts of the plant that are in the most active stage of growth, whether it is the sprout, the emerging rosette of leaves, the stem or the flower, the fruit or the seed, these being the repository of the plant's most vital energies. The third rule, which I consciously abide by every time I gather wild asparagus, is to pick a plant only where it breaks off naturally in your hand. This not only ensures that you won't end up eating the tough, fibrous parts , but is also generally the optimal place where new growth can emerge, such that the plant and the picker effectively sustain one another.

While gathering each variety of wild plant has its charms, as far as I'm concerned, there is nothing more enjoyable on a sunny winter day than to amble across the hills in search of wild asparagus. The billowy, thorny asparagus bushes grow in the vicinity of Tabor oaks, in some of the most magically beautiful forested terrain this land has to offer. The oak trees are bare, but underfoot is a riot of winter growth, blazing with wildflowers which often emerge right out of the crevices in mossy limestone boulders.

My attention is torn between the exquisite beauty of the winter landscape and the special focus needed to spot the tall, thin stalks of asparagus camouflaged amidst the foliage. Sometimes they emerge straight up out of the ground like little missiles, or else snake gracefully skyward, often to shoulder-height. It is no wonder the Bedouins believe that wild asparagus is nature's Viagra.

While the traditional Bedouin cooking method for wild asparagus is chopped in an omelet, we often enjoy the wild stalks steamed, so that their flavor, slightly more bitter and complex than the cultivated variety, can fully benefit from that most flattering dressing for winter greens—a drizzle of olive oil, a squeeze of lemon and a sprinkle of salt. On my gathering walks, I have come to pick only as many stalks as I can hold in one hand—which turns out to be the perfect serving size for two.

Euell Gibbons, in his seminal guide for foragers, *Stalking the Wild Asparagus*, described how, as a young man, he sat and stared at the elusive plant, internalizing its features until his eye was trained to distinguish it from the surrounding growth. After years of practice, I have also developed asparagus hunter's vision, passing my gaze lightly over each billowy bush, scanning for a sign of thicker vertical growth. Like snowflakes, each asparagus stalk has its own character—in color ranging from lime green to deep purple, in girth, as slender as a piece of spaghetti but never wider than a pencil, and the style with which it emerges into the world, ramrod straight or curling within the bush, so that you have to delicately insert your hand between the thorns to extract it.

Lately it has become more difficult to find wild asparagus—many more people have discovered the attraction of the hunt, including the Thai agricultural workers employed by local farmers. But if the competition in this area gets too stiff, I know there are plenty of other picking grounds to discover.

Asparagus Omelet

For 2 diners

Finely chop a bunch of wild asparagus. If wild asparagus isn't available, domesticated asparagus can be substituted. Sautee with chopped onion until the asparagus takes on a deep color. Mix four eggs in a cup, then pour them over the greens. Season with salt and pepper and cook until the eggs are set.

Mandrake the Magician

Once, at the time of the wheat harvest, Reuben came upon some mandrakes in the field and brought them to his mother Leah. Rachel said to Leah, "Please give me some of your son's mandrakes." But she said to her, "Was it not enough for you to take away my husband, that you would also take my son's mandrakes?" Rachel replied, "I promise, he shall lie with you tonight, in return for your son's mandrakes." When Jacob came home from the field in the evening, Leah went out to meet him and said, "You are to sleep with me, for I have hired you with my son's mandrakes."

Genesis 30:14-16

The mandrake grows wild in the fields and hills of the Galilee—I often encounter it on winter walks, easily identifiable by its cheery, purple flowers in a ground-hugging bouquet of wrinkly leaves. These blossoms have only the mildest smell, yet in the late autumn when they bloom, bees swarm from kilometers away to wallow in their pollen and consummate the fertilization process. Within months, clusters of fruit appear, like shiny green cherry tomatoes. By the end of spring, just about at the time of the wheat harvest, the mature fruit has softened, sweetened and turned a deep yellow. Mandrakes look as tantalizingly poisonous as they actually are—

unless you know how to handle them.

Micha Linn, a resourceful octogenarian born and raised on Kibbutz Mishmar Haemek, learned the secret of eating mandrakes as a youth while shepherding the kibbutz flock during school vacations. On blistering days between spring and summer, he would head for the tent of a neighboring Bedouin where they would relax in the shade while their respective herds grazed in peace. When the shepherds were thirsty, the Bedouin host would head off into the field and return with a handful of mandrakes. After peeling them and carefully removing the troublesome seeds, the two would refresh themselves with the juicy, sweet-sour fruit.

It was on just one of those blazing early summer days that I headed to the edge of the Jezreel Valley to visit Micha Linn at his kibbutz. As we sat together in the cinderblock storeroom that serves as his workshop, Linn reminisced over fifty years of labor in the kibbutz factory and fields. Yet it was only after he retired, he recalled, that the long-forgotten fruit from the past resurfaced in his imagination. The mandrake, it occurred to him, could lend itself nicely to fermentation. In his new leisure time, Linn apprenticed himself to a local winemaker and learned the technique for distilling fruit liqueur.

Linn poured us each a plastic shot glass of the syrupy pale yellow drink, which was sweet and aromatic and went straight to my head. As I sipped, Linn described how he ferries the ripe fruit through the processes of peeling, mashing, straining, fermenting and bottling. The bright orange pulp of the fruit passes twice through fine cheesecloth to ensure that not a single toxic seed is missed. "I'm not interested in killing anyone," he pointed out. In a single season, Linn produces about a thousand eight-ounce bottles.

Despite his rigorous precautionary measures and laboratory tests that confirm its safety, Linn has not been able to get a permit from the Israeli Ministry of Health to market his product. At this point, the bottles of liqueur can only be obtained at his kibbutz workroom, by special appointment only.

Linn is cultivating hundreds of mandrake plants in large, plastic barrel planters, ample enough to accommodate their legendary root, which can reach up to six feet in length and, when split down the middle, resembles the legs and torso of a human body. Ancient and medieval sources attributed magical powers to the mandrake root. According to one legend, anyone pulling up a mandrake by its root would die within 24 hours; the only way around this was to tie a horse or dog to the plant and let it do the dirty work. Linn reckons he has extracted so many mandrakes that at this point they are actually lengthening his days.

The Hebrew name for mandrakes—*dudaim*—alludes to the fruit of lovers. From the context of their appearance in ancient tomb paintings, it seems that the Egyptians believed in the mandrake's properties for enhancing ardor at least a millennium before the Bible was written. Rabbinic literature, expanding on the story of Jacob and his wives, deemed the coveted mandrake an inducer of fertility. At the devoutly secular Kibbutz Mishmar Haemek, Micha Linn was unaware of any of this.

That is, until the Orthodox customers started to appear. Word of the mandrake elixir began to spread in the Orthodox Jewish communities, and soon returning customers began to relate stories of how drinking the liqueur had resolved their problems of "sperm fatigue" and led to conception after everything else had failed. One rabbi from a city in the center of the country visits periodically, buying several cartons of the liqueur at a time.

Linn doesn't believe any of that. It's not what it does to you, he claims, but what it makes you want to do. He suggests that both partners drink a glass before dinner and another before retiring. The rest, he says, is up to nature.

Manakish

One rainy winter morning, Maryam and Emna invited me over to Bosmat Tabun for a visit. When I arrived, Emna was in the middle of preparing *manakish*. Sitting on the floor, she rolled out balls of dough, then set each flat circle of pita bread on a folded sheet spread on the carpet. When all the dough was flattened into disks, she plugged an ingenious aluminum cooking device into a wall socket. It looked like a combination of an old popcorn popper and an electric griddle, with the heating element on the inside of the top half, which screwed onto a deep lower container. Once it was hot, she took a round of dough, spooned a generous dollop of *zaatar* mixture in olive oil on top and spread it over the entire surface with the back of the spoon, then put the round of bread to cook on top of the griddle. After about three minutes, before the dough was entirely baked, she scooped the pita off the griddle, unscrewed the top part and slipped the pita into the lower pot to continue baking. A minute later, she removed it, crispy and bubbly hot, ready to eat.

We sat sipping coffee alongside our fresh *manakish*, sliced into delicate triangles like pizza—the sweet hot drink blending wonderfully with the mossy-sour granularity of the *zaatar*. I told the women about a new spot I'd found for picking *selek*. This would be our third winter making *ftayir* and I was hoping we could coordinate a time to pick the *selek* we would use. I asked Maryam's daughter, a high school senior, if she wanted to come along to pick with us, and she gave me an incredulous look. "These kids aren't interested in wild greens," Maryam sighed. "Sometimes when I serve *ellet* or *hubeisa*, they'll ask me 'what are you doing, putting us out to pasture?'"

Who wants to pick edible wild plants any more? The stigma of poverty and of being "old-fashioned" hovers in the contemporary consciousness. And why bother? These days, when *ellet, zaatar* and other wild plants have been cultivated and are readily available from greengrocers in any Arab village, people can buy their greens and eat them too.

Yet, even as sensibilities change and real estate development and herbicides diminish the best areas for picking, there will still be those who return to their favorite spots year after year to gather edible wild plants, out of nostalgia for the old ways and the old flavors, or for the sheer joy of spending a bright winter day outdoors, extending one's gaze and hands downward to receive what the earth is offering. I know I will be one of them.

FELLAHEEN

Beit Netufa Valley—*Sahel Batof*

The Grasses of the Field

But your food shall be the grasses of the field; Genesis 3:18

Dozens of varieties of wild grasses make up the spontaneous, natural cover of the Galilee hillsides. The thin rocky soil, erratic seasonal rainfall and blistering spring heat waves evidently suit them. The growth and ripening of both the wild grasses and their cultivated relatives define the shifting color scheme of our landscape—radiant green at the height of winter, bleaching to golden straw by the summer solstice, then settling into dusty, exhausted brown before the first winter rains.

On a spring walk through the fields, I grabbed the spiky towhead on a stalk of wild grass and after a quick upward pull, held all the spikelets in a bunch in my hand. Ron explained that the long, tiny-barbed frond on each one shows that it is barley—its Hebrew name, *seora*, literally means hairy. I remembered my small children and their friends pulling wild barley tops in the same way, hurling the spikelets at each other, then counting how many caught onto their shirts to predict the number of children they would have. Almost tempted to throw my handful of barley at Ron, I tossed it into the wind instead, preferring any effect on future progeny to remain in the cereal world.

Grains, particularly the varieties of barley and wheat indigenous to this part of the Middle East, are stocked with starches, protein and other nutrients. Thousands of years before they were cultivated, these cereals in their wild form provided the Stone Age hunters and gatherers in these parts with a plentiful source of food, but only after the hidden kernel of grain inside was plucked from the sturdy, protective spikelet that is the plant's vehicle for propagation. Ears of wild grain are significantly smaller and more delicate than the domesticated and hybrid super-grains grown today, so the process of gathering and collecting the kernels must have been particularly labor-intensive—yet not disproportionately so, considering that hunters and gatherers spent almost every waking moment procuring the ingredients for their next meal.

The cultivation of grain across the Fertile Crescent took place over thousands of years, culminating sometime around the 8th century BCE and ushering in the transition of hunting and gathering societies into settled agricultural communities. Grains offered the unique advantage of being an easily storable protein source, and with the availability of a surplus of food, energies could be shifted from staving off hunger towards uniquely human endeavors.

By my reckoning, if the two tips of the Fertile Crescent are Mesopotamia and the Nile, then the Galilee was right in the middle of the domestication action. I've read about the first grindstone that was conclusively proven to have crushed wheat some 23,000 years ago, plucked from the mud of the Sea of Galilee and sent to the laboratories of the Smithsonian Institute. Further downstream, relics from a primordial agricultural settlement were unearthed from the silty banks of the Yarmuk River, including shards of some of the earliest pottery jars ever made for storing grain, and river stones carved to serve as tools for harvesting and processing it. Other stones discovered there were fashioned into slit-eyed fertility goddesses that were buried in the crop rows, or incised with cryptic striations, possibly an iconic inventory system.

Yet another Galilee-wheat milestone was set in June 1906, when the botanist Aaron Aaronsohn identified wild emmer—the mother of all cultivated wheat—growing out of a crack in a limestone boulder on a hillside overlooking the Sea of Galilee. With this discovery, Aaronsohn concluded a heated professional search among European botanists for the original wild predecessor of cultivated wheat.

Wheat and barley are exceptionally nutritious and also versatile—the kernels can be roasted, cooked like porridge, or ground into flour which, when mixed with water and left to interact with airborne yeasts, produces a dough that is ideally suited for baking into bread. From these primeval beginnings, straight on through to the advent of the carbohydrate-free Atkin's Diet, bread was, and in many places still remains, the sun around which daily meals revolve.

Amin Abu Raya

You shall eat old grain long stored, and you shall have to clear out the old to make room for the new. Leviticus 26:10

Who is misken (pitiable)? He whose flour has spilled in a field of thorns.
Fellah saying

Until the 1950s and 60s, when the new Israeli cooperative farming communities and advanced agro-industrial methods transformed the agricultural landscape, *fellaheen* were cultivating wheat using techniques not much different from the Iron Age farming methods described in the Bible. This dramatic juxtaposition of old and new within such a compact geography and recent chronology, I found to be astounding. I decided to learn more about the culture and traditions of the Galilee *fellaheen*, particularly when it came to growing wheat. One spring morning, I drove north to Sakhnin—a city of about 25,000 residents at the border between the Lower and Upper Galilees—to visit the Museum of Palestinian Arab Tradition and Culture.

Amin Abu Raya, the museum's director, met me at the entrance to a historic stone compound set high on a steep hill. A trim, handsome man in his early 50s with graying temples and a Clark Gable mustache, Abu Raya exuded an air of weariness that came from the constant struggle to keep his institution afloat, and the museum had the dusty, faded look of chronic under-funding. Its modest collection includes examples of the rustic hand-hewn plows, pitchforks, threshing sleds and other agricultural equipment once used by the *fellaheen*, traditional household implements and a room lined with showcases displaying the ankle-length, embroidered women's dresses whose cross-stitch patterns encode the garments' origins and functions. A traditional *madafeh*, or salon, where the village leader or household head once received guests, is reproduced, with mannequins propped up in their places around the room according to social hierarchy.

We sat in Abu Raya's office off the courtyard of the museum and sipped black coffee as he explained how wheat permeated almost every aspect of the *fellaheen*'s world. Over several hours, systematically working his way through a pack of cigarettes, he shared with me the details of a way of life he can remember, but which no longer exists. Until the British Mandate, he explained, when municipal education systems were first instituted, most Palestinian *fellaheen* were unable to read and write, and the national culture was largely vested in a rich oral tradition. For just about every aspect of the agricultural cycle, the weather and the conditions of the earth, it seemed, Abu Raya knew a saying, parable or song that embellished it.

When the winter rains came on full force, he recounted, and the ground became too muddy to work in, the *fellah* had time to rest. This interlude was called "*el ejharath*" from the word "bald" or "smooth." The work of weeding the fields offered added compensation, as the edible wild plants offered an important nutritional supplement in this cold, rainy season. In March, when the lingering winter chill kept the old people from venturing outdoors, this was the season that "they had to burn their dowry chests to keep warm." By the end of the month, if there hadn't been a devastating drought or torrential rains, the *fellah* knew it was time to "tell his horse to get ready because spring had come." If rain hadn't been forthcoming, however, the old people and young children would appeal directly to divine authority, marching in procession through the village beating drums and carrying cloth flags, calling out to Allah to "bring down the rain—we have no food to eat."

By the end of the fifth month, when the wheat was mature but still green, a small part of the crop—about five percent, Abu Raya estimated—was harvested to be roasted and made into *freekeh*. Roasted green wheat not only offered the pleasure of tasting the season's first fruit, but if the previous year's harvest had been poor, the arrival of the new, green grain signaled the end of hunger for that year.

Barley, easier to cultivate, quicker to ripen, but more difficult to digest, was grown for animal feed. Already in Roman times, barley loaves were the food of the poor and slaves. In his autobiographical novel *Arabesques*, Anton Shammas describes one lean year from his childhood in the Western Galilee village of Fassuta, when the wheat had run out in the store room, the new crop wasn't ripe enough for an early harvest, and the family resorted to eating from the barley stored for the animals.

Just before the harvest, women would go into the field and pick 14 long stalks of wheat with which to weave a special fertility charm, representing the seven fat years and seven lean years of Joseph's prophetic dream. An exquisite example is on display in the museum.

When you reap the harvest of your land, you shall not reap all the way to the edges of your field, or gather the gleanings of your harvest... you shall leave them for the poor and the stranger... Leviticus 19:9-10

By June, the wheat was ready to be harvested, a cooperative, family affair. Abu Raya described how the harvesters would line up, man, woman and child, with the most senior family member leading the work. Arranged in a line an arm's length apart, they would enter the field on their knees, their right hands wielding the sickles, their left hands gathering the cut stalks, steadily advancing and leaving piles of cut wheat behind them. These were bundled together and then carried to the threshing floor at the outskirts of the town. At this point, according to Islamic law, the old women and the poor were allowed to enter the field and glean whatever grain had fallen from the stalks.

On the threshing floor, the wheat was spread "like the veil of a bride." A heavy wooden threshing sledge, its underside studded with chunks of basalt stone, was hitched to a mule, bull or other beast and dragged over the wheat to separate the grains from the hulls. Abu Raya broke into a grin as he recalled the joy of riding on that sledge as a child. Then, using a wooden pitchfork, the men tossed the wheat into the air, standing perpendicular to the direction of the wind so that the heavy grains would fall onto the threshing floor to be collected and cleaned by the women. The chaff would blow off onto separate piles according to its weight. The first pile was used as food for camels, donkeys and mules, the second pile for sheep, goats and cows, and the third was mixed with clay to reinforce it as a building material. What blew over onto the neighbor's threshing floor was beyond the pale.

He will take a tenth part of your grain and vintage and give it to
his eunuchs and courtiers. 1 Samuel 8:15

Once the grain was collected, cleaned and weighed, the various taxes, payments and tributes were deducted. An assessor from the Turkish authorities would show up for the day of reckoning to collect the official government tax in wheat. Then the local expenses had to be covered—a tax to the village *imam;* payment of any outstanding debt to the grocer and butcher; an advance to the barber for a year of haircuts and shaves (two *seah*s, or the equivalent of about 12 kilos of wheat per family member); and the tithe for the poor, as dictated by the Koran.

What remained, called the *muni,* went into the storeroom and had to feed the *fellah's* entire extended family until the next year's harvest, taking into account the possibility of a future drought and setting aside enough seeds for planting for the following year. About ten percent of the wheat would be turned into bulgur—that is, boiled, dried and ground in three different grades. The coarsest would be cooked with lentils to make *mejadra,* the middle grind would be used for preparing *kubbeh,* and the finest for preparing *tabouleh* and for dishes eaten with *leben.*

The remainder would be saved to be milled into flour for the daily task of baking the loaves of flat pita bread that were an extension of each diner's hand at every meal. Perpetuating the millennia-old local diet, the *fellah* subsisted on fresh bread and whatever it could be dipped into—olive oil and *zaatar* or a stew of lentils, chickpeas, *malukhiya* , wild greens, or *labaneh.* The eating of meat was usually reserved for the celebrations of births, weddings and other festive occasions.

All roads lead to the wheat mill. Fellah saying

Until the advent of steam-powered mills at the end of the 19th century, the *fellah* would take his wheat to a water-powered flour mill, and the ruins of these stone structures, and the channels and dams that fed into them, can still be found hidden in the undergrowth bordering the dormant streambeds of Nahal Ammud, Nahal Tsalmon and other natural but long since dried-up waterways in the Galilee. In the early 1930s, steam-powered flour mills began to be installed in towns and villages.

Today, except for the crops of a small number of *fellaheen* whose yields serve the needs of the local Arab markets, the vast majority of the wheat grown in the Galilee comes from large agro-industrial farms, and is destined either as food for the cows in the region's many dairies or the silos of government-regulated granaries. For almost everyone outside of the Arab sector, flour comes in a paper kilo package purchased at a grocery store, comprised almost entirely of grain imported from the United States or the FSU. Plots of land where *fellaheen* once grew wheat have largely been replanted with olive trees, which require vastly less labor and produce a far more cost-effective commodity. And with the introduction of the mechanical combine, in one lifetime and after thousands of years, the threshing floor has almost entirely lost its purpose.

Kalí—Parched Golden Wheat

*At mealtime, Boaz said to her, "Come over here and partake
of the meal… He handed her roasted grain, and she ate
her fill and had some left over.* Ruth 2:14

Amin Abu Raya remembers *kaliye*—roasted grains of
wheat—as a favorite harvest time snack. Wheat can be
roasted, or "parched" as it is often referred to in Biblical
translations, when it is partially ripe and still green, or fully
ripe and golden. The roasting process (*liklot* in Hebrew)
relates to the Biblical Hebrew name of this food—*kalí*, or in
Arabic, *kaliye*. *Kalí*, Boaz's love offering to Ruth, is delicious
eaten fresh and hot—and it reminds me of the crunchy, un-
popped kernels at the bottom of the popcorn bowl.

Heat a tablespoon of olive oil in a frying pan. Add 1 cup of
wheat kernels and roast them for a minute or two. Add salt
and eat immediately.

Kfar Manda

*…but the land you are about to cross into and possess, a land of hills
and valleys, soaks up its water from the rains of heaven…. I will grant
the rain for your land in season, the early rain and the late.*

Deuteronomy 11:11-14

The Lower Galilee is spread across a series of vast sweeping valleys
bordered by low-rising hills and mountain ranges. The flat valley land
soaks up the winter rains and stores the moisture with remarkable
efficiency, and the runoff from the hills packs the soil with nutrients.
These intensely fertile valleys have been cultivated for thousands of
years, most probably since the advent of organized agriculture. Indifferent to the loyalties of those who till it, the land produces or with-
holds its yield, answering only to the sun and the clouds.

Here, the topography, climate and local crops synchronize
across two growing seasons. Fall/winter is occupied with the cultivation of grain, typically wheat, but also barley, as well as legumes
such as chickpeas and fava beans. Grains are particularly suited to
the seasonal rains and rich valley earth of the Lower Galilee.

To produce a substantial crop of grain, there must be rain
early enough in the season to allow for sowing the seeds in a timely

fashion, rains in the middle of the season, alternated with significant stretches of dry, sunny days, to nurture the young plants without drowning or parching them, and later rains, which are absolutely critical at the stage when the kernels are forming inside the ears. Springtime heat waves are essential for the final ripening, yet if they come before the grains are mature, they can result in blight. Any disturbance in the balance of rain and sunlight can have a disastrous impact on the final harvest.

In spring/summer, after the grain is harvested, enough moisture remains in the valleys' water table to support a season of vegetable cultivation—traditionally squashes, melons, and cucumbers—with no more watering than what is drawn from the earth and the morning dew.

Today, when irrigation lines cross most of these valleys, the repertoire of crops has expanded to include corn, tomatoes, broccoli and other imported newcomers. But the original growing seasons continue to dictate the rhythm of life for those who still practice some semblance of traditional agriculture.

• • •

Since ancient times, human settlements have been established at the crease between the valleys and the slopes behind them. Precious agricultural land was not wasted, and the back-lying hills were planted with fruit trees, olive trees and vines, to be harvested during the summer and fall. The hills also provided grazing space for sheep, goats and other animals, at a safe remove from the cultivated fields, as well as gathering grounds for wild herbs, carobs and firewood. But always, the deciding factor for where to settle has been an accessible spring or other source of water.

Kfar Manda, located at the western edge of the Beit Netufa Valley, known in Arabic as *Sahel Batof,* is such a settlement. Today it is a sprawling, densely populated and economically depressed Arab village-turned-town. But only a few generations ago, it was a small village of *fellaheen,* whose lives revolved around working the valley land. Kfar Manda was once renowned for its wheat and its watermelons. Because the crops there were raised *baal*—without irrigation— the watermelons were prized for their particularly intense flavor. Today, the mention of those watermelons—*batikh el batof*—draws a deep sigh out of those who remember them, particularly when they are faced with one of today's oversized, watered-down, seedless varieties. The wheat grown in Kfar Manda is now hybrid durum, offering yields that no commercial farmer can turn his back on.

Abu Zaki

I first came to Kfar Manda following a sesame trail. A friend who produces and markets fair-trade olive oil and *zaatar*, and prefers to purchase the sesame seeds she uses in her *zaatar* mixture locally, invited me to join her on a visit to her supplier. Imported sesame almost entirely dominates the Israeli market, she explained. But Abu Zaki of Kfar Manda is one of the few farmers left in the Galilee who still grows this most ancient of crops.

This was an invitation I was thrilled to accept, and on the appointed morning, I parked my car at the entrance to the village and waited for my friend to pick me up. It was the first time I'd ever entered Kfar Manda, and I wondered what kind of reception we, two Jewish women, would encounter. Kfar Manda was the scene of some of the worst violence during the Second Intifada, and even after a decade, for most Jews, it was simply off their radar.

Once I got into my friend's car, she told me she'd only been to the village a few times before, and we tentatively made our way past the homes, shops and vegetable stores that line the main street, to reach the center of town. At the main traffic circle, Abu Zaki was waiting for us—a tall, broad and deeply tanned older man with striking black eyes, wearing a pure white *keffiye* held in place with a black band like a halo.

Abu Zaki climbed into the car and directed us off the main road and onto a side street that led straight to the agricultural fields of the *Batof*. His parcels of land were planted with a variety of crops, and we passed dusty lines of peppers and claw-like okra before we came to a pair of long rows of sesame plants.

Sesame grows on tall, wiry bushes, with long thin leaves and multiple pods about the length of my littlest finger. When the pods are dry enough, they split open and disperse their sesame seeds. For the farmer, the challenge is to harvest the pods before they reach that stage and the season's investment is gone with the wind. On this particular summer day, the pods were still tightly shut and Abu Zaki estimated that it would be a few more weeks before he'd be harvesting them.

We returned with Abu Zaki to the center of the village and he invited us to his home for coffee, just a short distance from the main circle. We sat on plastic chairs in the paved front courtyard, joined by several old women who served coffee and fresh fruit. My friend spoke Arabic with them, while my stomach twisted in awe and shame. If she could learn Arabic, then why couldn't I?

I whispered to her to please ask Abu Zaki if he would be willing to meet with me one day so I could talk to him about his life as a farmer here. He seemed rather puzzled by my request, but agreed. Because he wasn't so comfortable speaking Hebrew, though, he preferred if his nephew, Malek, would come along and translate. I wrote down Malek's telephone number and we left.

Back to Abu Zaki

A few weeks later, I was back at Abu Zaki's home, this time with Malek as my escort. A slight, serious man in his early 40s, with shorn graying hair and large, deep-set eyes, Malek had agreed to join me on a Friday morning—a day he wasn't working—to visit his uncle. I picked him up, along with his 11-year-old son Fadel, at the entrance to the village, and he directed the way to Abu Zaki's home.

Again we sat on the plastic garden chairs in the front courtyard with Abu Zaki and the two elderly women, who Malek explained were his two wives. The women, who I guessed to be in their seventies, wore the floor-length dresses and scarf head coverings that identified them as devout village women. When the second wife was widowed, Abu Zaki took her in; as a formidable landholder and senior figure in the village, he had the standing and means to support another spouse, and the relationship between them all seemed amicable. A plate of fresh fruit was placed on a table between us and Abu Zaki pressed a fig into my hand.

We spoke about Kfar Manda as he remembered it as a child during the time of the *"Anglizi,"* when the village had about 700 residents and all the families were *fellaheen*. Even if you didn't own your own land, he explained, you worked in the harvest and were paid in wheat, which was the only money they had. He remembers when the seeds were sown by hand and the fields were plowed behind a bull. During the wheat harvest, they worked 12-hour days for weeks on end, the women cutting the wheat with sickles, and the men collecting the cut grain and transporting it to the threshing floor.

In the new State of Israel, as other *fellaheen* were losing their land to the state, Abu Zaki was able to keep a portion of his, and continued to farm. But the agricultural landscape as they knew it was turned upside down. The new state banked in hard cash, and wheat was no longer acceptable currency. The nearby kibbutzim and moshavim, with their agro-industry based on modern equipment and state-of-the-art farming technologies, were dominating the local markets, and reaching out overseas.

Abu Zaki and other local *fellaheen* tried to adapt to this new reality. In the 1960s, he told me, he and another farmer pooled resources to buy their first tractor. One year, he remembers, the entire Beit Netufa valley was planted with tomatoes, to supply a new tomato processing plant. Then the price of tomatoes plummeted and the plant closed down. When a sugar factory was built nearby, they switched to growing sugar beets. But that factory went out of business too.

Finally, Abu Zaki went back to growing wheat in the winter and vegetables in the summer. The market for his produce is in Kfar Manda and the nearby Arab villages. A significant number of customers still prefer to buy wheat in grain form, and there is a mill in the village where they can take it to be ground into flour. These days he grows durum wheat varieties which yield about four times what the old varieties could produce. I asked him if anyone still uses the old strains of wheat, and he looked at me as if I'd asked if anyone still plowed with a bull.

"But now, everything has changed," Abu Zaki said. "There isn't a single cow, even a chicken, left in the village. Everything has to be bought." This seemed particularly unfortunate to me since I knew that in many Bedouin villages, families often kept sheep, goats and chickens. But his words stayed with me as I came to know Kfar Manda well enough to sense that something vital was missing at its core.

"Come with me," he said. "There's something I'd like to show you." We left the courtyard and headed a few steps down the street towards the center of the village. Then Abu Zaki stepped off the street and onto a path that led into a walled open courtyard, where large aluminum trays of bulgur, and tarps covered with *malukhiye* leaves were drying in the sun. "This is the house I grew up in," he explained. He opened a weathered wooden door at the far end of the courtyard and we stepped inside, into one large dim room and another lifetime. "This is where our entire family lived and slept. The animals were kept over there in the corner, separated by a partition." He gestured up to a high loft. "That's where we stored the sacks of grain, jars of oil and other dry foods."

The concrete floor and thick walls kept the room cool despite the intense summer heat outside. "At first, the house was built of wood and covered with clay. In the 1950s we reinforced it with concrete." There was a jumbled collection of old couches and chairs in the room, and a cold coffee pot and emptied cups rested on a tray on the table. This, it turned out, was the domain of Abu Zaki's first wife.

Suddenly, the voice of the muezzin filled the air and Abu Zaki hurriedly took his leave, heading off to the mosque. Malek and I made our way back to the car. "If only I could learn Arabic," I said, and sighed in frustration. "Well that's no problem," Malek said. "I'll teach you Arabic, and you can help me with my English."

Malek and Family

And so it was arranged. A week after my visit to Abu Zaki, I returned yet again to Kfar Manda, this time to Malek's family home, for my first Arabic lesson. I found the house at the top of a long, inclining road lined with shops, large stucco homes that typically housed several generations of a single family, with small paved yards crowding almost to the street, and one of the many mosques in the village. In front of one house, a cluster of men and women sat around a low table drinking coffee poured from a long-handled pot. Further on, inside a dark doorway, several men attended to the village's flour mill.

In front of Malek's home, a grape arbor shaded the narrow parking spot, and several lemon trees were obstinately surviving in a small space of packed earth. Under the neighbors' curious gaze, I climbed the outdoor stairs that led past one set of doors, to the second level of the house, where Malek, his wife Samakh, and their four children live.

In the small living room, Malek and I talked while Samakh, at least ten years younger than her husband, placed glasses of lemonade on the table with one hand, and fended off their energetic, one-year-old son with the other. She wore jeans and a stylish head covering, and with her shy smile looked almost like a teenager.

Malek's youngest daughter, a sassy and exuberant three-year-old, was recruited to help with our lesson. We practiced the words for eyes, nose and mouth—as she gleefully pointed to each one. "Bring me the spoon," I recited. "Take the spoon." "Put the spoon on the table." Soon, there was a knock on the door and Malek's parents, Abu Malek and Um Malek, entered the living room, having climbed the stairs from their apartment on the floor below. Because he is the oldest of the siblings, Malek explained to me, he has stayed in this house while new homes were built by the family for all his brothers.

Abu Malek, in his early eighties, is thin and slightly stooped, with white springy hair and large, gentle eyes that give him the air of a lamb. He extended a hand to me in welcome and addressed me in English. "How do you do?" Before he retired, Abu Malek taught high school English, Arabic and Hebrew, and was also the principal at the local school. Clearly pleased to practice his English, he recited lines from Shakespeare and nursery rhymes, and wanted to hear more about me.

Um Malek sat quietly by the kitchen table, and I could see where her son's dramatic eyes came from. Under her white head-scarf, affixed beneath her chin with a pin, her own eyes were a deep and stunning blue, and they glowed as she smiled at me in welcome. I noted to myself that marrying younger women seemed to be a family tradition. Um Malek is Abu Zaki's sister, and while her husband was always a schoolteacher, she grew up working in the fields and is a *fellah* in the truest sense. On that morning she had brought with her an armful of *malukhiye* and she began to systematically pluck the papery-thin, coin-sized leaves from the long, stiff stems. The leaves would be cooked, together with chicken and garlic, to create a bright green, somewhat gelatinous soup that is the traditional Friday afternoon lunch in most Kfar Manda homes. Abu Zaki is one of the largest growers and suppliers of *malukhiye* on the local market.

"Um Malek is always busy," Abu Malek explained, as he gazed at her affectionately. "She doesn't sit still for a minute." In the years I have come to know Um Malek, it's true I've almost never seen her idle. Either she is cleaning and sifting a huge tray of sesame seeds from her brother's field, or bulgur that she has prepared herself, boiling the grains of wheat, then drying them on the rooftop, which she will use to prepare Galilean *mejadra*. She dries *zaatar*, then crushes the leaves through a sieve to produce her own *dukka*—the village name for a spice mixture. She also collects and dries savory, mint and chamomile flowers to use as medicinal teas. In the summer, she cleans okra, rolls grape leaves around rice filling, and dries *malukhiye* leaves and crushes them into powder so there will be a supply of this staple during the winter months. During the olive harvest she works in her brother's olive grove, earning an extra allotment of oil for the family. In the winter, she leaves the house early in the morning for long walks, returning with bags of *luf*, *selek*, *ellet* and wild mushrooms, which Abu Malek calls *lakhem el fakir*—the meat of the poor. "Then we feast without spending a penny," he proudly explained.

Um Malek doesn't speak Hebrew and, again, Malek was pressed into translating. I wanted to know what she was saying, what foods she was preparing, and how she cooked them. Malek explained to her that I was interested in traditional foodways, and I described how I enjoyed picking *selek*, *ellet* and *hilayon*. She was as amused and delighted as if someone from Mars had dropped into the living room, and was showing that, on their planet, these plants exist as well. When I visit I like to bring her pomegranates and pecans from our garden, or a jar of our home-made olives, and she sends me home with a pot of *malukhiyeh* or a bag of okra.

Galilean *Mejadra*

And Esau said to Jacob, "Give me some of that red stuff to gulp down, for I am famished"... Genesis 25:30

Mejadra is most commonly known as a Middle Eastern dish pairing lentils and rice. In the Galilee, where wheat was king and rice an exotic import, the lentils were matched with coarsely ground bulgur instead. The "red stuff" that Esau hankered for is generally considered to have been lentil stew. Galilean *mejadra* is distinguished by its ruddy color, derived from onions that are bronzed in a long and copious olive oil bath. *Mejadra*, served with *leben* and a little fresh salad, is Galilee Arab comfort food.

Cook 1/2 cup of small black lentils in 4 cups boiling water until soft. In the meantime, sauté 4 chopped onions in 1/3 cup olive oil until very brown but not burned. Once the onions are brown, add 2 cups of water to the pan and stir well. When the water has almost boiled away, add 2 cups of coarsely ground bulgur and mash it into the onions with a wooden spoon. When the lentils are soft, add them, plus as much as their cooking water as you need, to more than cover the bulgur. The type of lentils and bulgur used, and how much water is left in the onions, will determine how much liquid to add. You can always add more liquid or let the excess cook away. When the bulgur is cooked through, season with salt to taste.

Abu Malek

As the weeks went by, my presence in the house came to be a routine. The children would emerge from their rooms when I came, and I brought books for them to practice their English with. The novelty of my visits wore off for the youngest daughter as well, and she preferred to play with her toys and her little brother than to engage in our language games. Malek was often busy with phone calls, and it was Abu Malek who took up the challenge of teaching this foreign woman Arabic.

I had bought a book for learning Arabic, and each week, Abu Malek and I would go through our lesson. He clearly looked forward to our weekly meetings and so did I, not so much for the lessons themselves, but for the convivial conversation afterwards. The lessons progressed slowly, and as I read the dialogue out loud, he'd correct my pronunciation again and again, explaining with exasperation that I was inadvertently expressing a completely different word. Mispronouncing the word for zucchini, for example, could be a source of tremendous embarrassment, he insisted. With equal frustration I had to admit that the differences between the words were entirely imperceptible to my ear.

For as much as I was progressing with the book, I was finding Arabic almost impossible to master, in large part because of the pronunciation. For native English speakers, most of the language-forming work is carried out in the front of the mouth, by the tongue and teeth. Arabic emerges, airborne, from the back of the throat. I began to despair of ever coaxing my diaphragm and facial musculature into producing understandable Arabic speech.

After we put the book aside, it was time to talk about food. I asked Abu Malek to tell me some of the many sayings in Arabic that have to do with farming and cooking. I learned "During watermelon season, you don't need to cook," and "During fig season, you don't need to make bread dough." That "he who has dried figs eats with both hands," and that "a nut won't give anything until it's broken." And of course, that every pot has its lid and that the apple doesn't fall far from the tree.

For all my lack of progress, I love using the Arabic words I've learned, like the word for parsley—*bakdoness*—which sounds so regal, and for orange—*bortukali*—that makes me think of Moorish traders in the Iberian Peninsula. Like a polite American, I use *shukran* and *afwan*—thank you and your welcome—liberally. And then there are the blessings that are a part of every greeting: *Salam adeki*—Bless your hands; *Ya tiku el affiyeh*—May you have strength; and *Ahalan usahalan*—extended in welcome, with a wish that your way be as free and unobstructed as an open valley.

Ultimately, I have found that my efforts are best spent learning key, useful phrases. *Sharafna*, for example, is a very polite way to say I am honored to meet you. When I use this word, particularly when introduced to older people, they are delighted. I have also learned several forms of hello and goodbye—and the answers to the inevitable questions: that I live in Alonei Aba, that I have a husband and two sons, that I come from America, and that I have lived here for twenty-five years. That I speak a little bit of Arabic, and that I am studying the language.

It's remarkable what a long way these expressions go. Beyond their intrinsic meaning, they say that I have made the effort to meet the other person on their ground, in their language, where they are comfortable. Even when they are pronounced wrong, these words deliver a powerful message.

One Thousand and One Meals

… he (Abraham) was sitting at the entrance of the tent as the day grew hot. Looking up, he saw three men standing near him. As soon as he saw them, he ran from the entrance of the tent to greet them and, bowing to the ground, he said, "My lords, if it please you, do not go on past your servant…. let me fetch a morsel of bread that you may refresh yourselves; then go on—seeing that you have come your servant's way." Genesis 18:1-5

Many times, after our lesson, Abu Malek would tell me Arab tales and legends or stories from the Koran. He always started out slowly, enunciating each word, but inevitably would get caught up in the tale, leaving me struggling to understand the Arabic, and somehow follow the plot line. Often we ended up falling back to Hebrew—the only language we comfortably shared in common.

In one of our conversations, I told Abu Malek about the story I'd just read in Genesis, where Abraham prepared a feast to welcome visiting angels. The foods in this first instance of hospitality in the Bible—cakes of fine flour, cheese and fresh meat—seemed to epitomize a local Bedouin meal for an honored guest. Abu Malek told me that there was a similar story in the Koran—except that, although *Ibrahim Avinu* offered the angels food, as celestial beings, they refused it. But there was another story about *Ibrahim Avinu* and hospitality, he explained, and went on to tell it.

One day, *Ibrahim* was sitting outside his tent when he saw an old man passing by. "Come and relax and refresh yourself," he called out to the old man. As they sat down to eat their meal, *Ibrahim* reminded the old man that first they had to give thanks to God for their food. "What God are you talking about?" the old man said. "I don't know about any God." *Ibrahim*, seeing that an infidel was in his midst, drove the old man out of his tent and sent him packing.

Soon afterwards *Ibrahim* heard God's voice addressing him. "Where is the old man?" he asked. "He's gone. I sent him away. He was a non-believer." "And how old do you think that man was?" God asked *Ibrahim*. "Oh, perhaps he was 70 or 80," *Ibrahim* replied. "Well", God answered. "If I've put up with him for that long, don't you think you could be patient with him for at least one meal?" *Ibrahim* realized his mistake, and ran after the old man, bringing him back to his tent. Again they sat down to eat. The old man asked *Ibrahim*, "Why did you come back to get me?" "God made me realize that I'd made a mistake", *Ibrahim* answered. "Well then", the old man replied. "I think I like this God of yours. Now tell me, what do we have to do to bless him?"

·   ·   ·

From a bookstore in Jerusalem, I bought an anthology of Arab folk tales collected from villages around the Galilee, and I brought it to share with Abu Malek. The stories were translated from Arabic to Hebrew, and the two languages were printed on facing pages. The storytellers were almost all men in their later years, Muslim, Druze and Christian, and there was a photo and short biography of each one. Abu Malek flipped through the pages intently, pointing with satisfaction when he recognized this storyteller and that one.

The stories describe events and legends drawn from the oral histories of the respective villages. In dramas small and grand, the characters exhibit faith and depravity, cunning and good fortune, generosity and modesty, courage and humility. Some of the tales offer just the briefest glimpse of a time and place that no longer exist. I left the book with Abu Malek, and it was waiting on the table for me when I returned the following week. Certain stories, he concluded, were more satisfying than others. But the collection was compelling enough to keep him reading non-stop over two days until he finished the last story.

Hospitality was a recurring theme in the stories, where men of stature are measured by how gracious they are, particularly to strangers and the unfortunate. With the help of the translation on the pages in front of us, we worked our way through one of the tales, from the village of Mghrar.

The story begins when a wealthy sheikh sees a beggar sitting under a tree. He tells his servant to call the poor man in to his home, then sends him to slaughter a sheep and invite all the distinguished men of the village for a meal. When they ask their host what the occasion is for the feast, they are incredulous when he tells them it is in honor of the beggar. After all, he admonishes them, who knows if he isn't an angel sent by *Allah*, in disguise?

Time passes and the sheikh travels to another city. There, a distinguished-looking local man greets him by name and invites him and his entourage for a meal. Asked how he knows the visitor's name, the man replies that he will explain everything in due time.

When the visitors reach the man's home, the doorway is high and wide enough to accommodate a horse and rider. The mysterious host has slaughtered five sheep—one for each of his guests. After the meal, he reveals that he is, in fact, that same beggar who had been hosted in the guest's home.

A discussion ensues. Who is more honorable? "You are", the guest exclaims to his host. "I only slaughtered one sheep and you served up five." "No", the host replies. "You are. I invited you knowing who you and your friends are. But you invited in a beggar."

They both had a point, I told Abu Malek. But the way I see it, extending hospitality to an anonymous stranger is an opportunity to recognize the sanctity of both the host and the guest. And it doesn't matter if it is five sheep or one, or even just a morsel of bread and a sip of cool water. It's the sharing between fellow spirits where holiness resides.

Sulkha

"Let us make a pact with you that you will not do us harm, just as we have not molested you but have always dealt kindly with you and sent you away in peace. From now on, be you blessed of the Lord!" Then he made for them a feast, and they ate and drank. Genesis 26:28

The institution of *sulkha* is still practiced in the Arab communities of the Galilee, to resolve conflicts between clans, traditionally when one clan member is harmed or murdered by another. In some cases, an entire clan is forced to leave its village over such a conflict and can only return once a *sulkha* agreement has been reached. The job of negotiating the *sulkha* traditionally falls on the most respected village elders. After the *sulkha* conditions are agreed upon and a fee is negotiated, in sums that generally represent a small fortune, the peace-making is consummated with a festive meal to which the entire village is invited.

Malek told me he had recently been to a *sulkha* meal hosted by the clan of a friend of his. Back in the 1970s, one of that friend's relatives had been assaulted by members of another clan and he had killed one of them in self-defense. Finally, after thirty years of living in exile in Kfar Manda, the friend and his family were able to return to their home village. I asked him what they ate at the *sulkha* meal. The usual, he replied. They slaughtered a few calves and served meat and rice. Enough food for several hundred guests. The menu, I understood, was beside the point. It was the act of sharing food that sealed the pact of peace.

I recalled one of the stories from the book of Arab folk tales, the only one related by a woman, from the village of Sakhnin. It was told to her by her mother, and the events took place during the British Mandate.

When a brawl broke out between members of the Abu Raya and the El Haleileh clans, all the men were rounded up by the police, arrested, and imprisoned in the olive press. In the meantime, the wise old Abu Raya women put their heads together and came up with a plan. That night they started to prepare *zalabiya* and all kinds of other sweets, in total silence so no one from the El Haleileh clan would guess what they were up to. They even wrapped the block of sugar they were chipping away at in cloth so that the sound wouldn't reach unwanted ears.

The next morning, all the Abu Raya women dressed in their finest clothing, as if they were going to a wedding. With their trays of sweets on their heads, they set out for the olive press. When the policeman guarding the prisoners saw the women in all their finery, he tried to chase them away. "No wedding today", he said. "Open the door," the leader of the women commanded. "Tell the men that we've brought a breakfast feast for everyone." The women laid out the array of confections, inviting all the prisoners and the guards to partake.

After they finished eating, the men told the guards, "We've

eaten together one meal from one platter. That means we've made peace with one another. Let us go home now."

Just then, the El Haleileh women showed up, each one carrying a modest meal for her imprisoned husband, brother or son. Their menfolk told them, "Go back. The clever Abu Raya women already feasted us and made peace. Now we are coming home."

I mentioned this story to Abu Malek as an example of how *sulkha* between clans was marked with a meal. He remembered the story well. But there's another point, he said. Those shrewd women from Sakhnin completely bypassed the entire *sulkha* process, saving everyone a fortune in time and money by making peace between the clans simply through having them share a meal of sweets.

The Well

"An Egyptian rescued us from the shepherds; he even drew water for us and watered the flock." He said to his daughters, "Where is he then? Why did you leave the man? Ask him in to break bread." Exodus 2:19

One day Abu Malek offered to take me for a walk in the historic heart of the village. It was an unusually grey and gloomy spring day, but we were undeterred, and cheerfully set off on our outing. Abu Malek, Malek, Fadel and I piled into my car and we made the three-minute drive down to the center of the village. On the way, Abu Malek pointed out an empty overgrown lot between several houses. That spot, he explained, was named for the good clay that is found there, which used to be collected for building walls and ovens. We parked in front of Abu Zaki's house, and he happened to be sitting alone outside in the front courtyard. "Come in and have coffee," he invited us. Abu Malek explained our mission and promised that we'd come back afterwards.

Our first stop was the village well—or what used to be the well. From Abu Zaki's, it was only a few yards away. Today, the site is in the center of a traffic circle, completely paved in stone, with a raised, massive, geometrically looming memorial for villagers who have lost their lives from 1938 on through the Second Intifada. A few shaggy palm trees share this platform. Where the spring once issued forth its waters, there was a low tangle of rusty pipes surrounded by trash.

"Up here is where the women used to gather water every day in jars to bring back to their houses," Abu Malek explained, describing a picture that was still clear in his memory. "And in the lower part of the pool, there was a trough where the animals would be watered. In those days, it wasn't customary for young men and women to speak to one another. So the only place that they could communicate—if only through shared glances—was at the well.

"There is a local legend that says, as it is written in the Koran, that after escaping from Egypt, young Moses came here to Kfar Manda, and it was at this well that he helped the daughters of the Midian priest to water their beasts. That's why they say this place is called 'Manda'. But those are just stories..."

Fat raindrops started to fall on us and we left the well behind, running to take cover in a small grocery store whose proprietor, Abu Ali, is a friend of Abu Malek's. As we ducked into the door, I noticed next to the storefront several round stones that I recognized as capitals from Roman columns, just sitting on the ground. "Look at those," I exclaimed, and Malek explained that when the traffic circle and monument were being built, these old relics had been removed from inside the well and someone had just left them there.

The store was tiny and jam-packed with foods and dry goods. Abu Ali arranged a few chairs for us between the refrigerator and the countertops. He poured each of us a small cup of hot ginger tea with honey and then, from a second thermos, offered sips of *saada*. This was where Abu Malek bought his newspaper every Friday, always lingering for coffee and conversation with Abu Ali. The rain hadn't let up and it was warm and convivial inside the store. Abu Malek explained who I was and the nature of our outing. I mustered some of my best Arabic expressions and tried them out on our host, to his great amusement.

· · ·

It is the season of the wheat harvest. I will pray to the Lord and He will send thunder and rain; then you will take thought and realize what a wicked thing you did in the sight of the Lord when you asked for a King.
1 Samuel 12:17

The rain stopped and, after a brief peek into the village's old mosque with its carpeted expanse empty between prayers, we headed back to Abu Zaki's for coffee and fresh baklava. I asked Abu Zaki what this late rain meant for his wheat crop, which should have been just about ready for harvesting. "No good," he said. "It will lay the wheat down." Later on, I saw what he meant. Large swaths had been pushed down onto their sides by the weight of the rainfall. The combine would now have a hard time harvesting those sections of the field, and if the wheat was already cut, the moisture in the mounded grain could end up causing it to rot.

On the drive home, Malek asked me if, after that modest little tour of the village center, anything had made an impression on me from what we had seen. "There's nothing there," he said dejectedly. "No awareness of preservation or history." Yet as bleak as the scene was, I was still elated. "I saw this place through your father's eyes," I explained, "and that was such a gift." Through his memories, the stories of Isaac and Rebecca, of Joseph, Leah and Rachel, of Moses and Tsippora, and of countless generations who had gathered water at that well had come to life.

FELLAHEEN

Nazareth

Ein Dor

You shall observe the Feast of Weeks, of the first fruits of the wheat
harvest; and the Feast of Ingathering at the turn of the year. Exodus 34:22

The archaeological museum at Kibbutz Ein Dor was offering a
wheat harvest activity for families during the Jewish holiday of
Shavuot and I marked it on my calendar. During Biblical times,
Shavuot celebrated the arrival of the wheat harvest, when the faithful were commanded to bring an offering of the freshly cut grain
to the Temple in Jerusalem. These days, even when most Jewish
holidays barely acknowledge their agricultural roots, here in Israel,
particularly among the agricultural cooperatives, Shavuot is still
celebrated as the festival of "first fruits."

I arrived at the museum a few minutes early, paid for my ticket,
and walked around the courtyard. There was a distinct fragrance
of freshly baking bread, and I followed my nose to a table where
several women were preparing pita bread in an outdoor oven. They
were middle-aged and Arab, although only two of the three were
wearing the traditional head covering of observant Muslim women.

Coming closer for a better look, I saw that what they were sell-
ing was no ordinary pita. Instead, on the table was a stack of dense,

golden brown flat breads, thickly studded with sesame, anise and nigella seeds, and decorated with a cheerful mandala pattern imprinted into the dough with a carved wooden mold. "I'll take one of those," I said. Then I asked the woman handling the dough—the one with the long black hair, broad smile and sparkling dark eyes— what this exquisite bread was called, and if I could take a photo of it. *Hubs el kaleb* she replied, explaining that *hubs* is the Arabic word for bread, and *kaleb*, for the wooden mold that decorates it. Her name was Balkees, she told me, just like the Queen of Sheba in the Koran. And permission to photograph she willingly gave, but on the condition that I send her a copy to the email address she wrote down in my notebook.

Golden-crusted and steamy, redolent of spices and densely crunchy, this was bread that couldn't be eaten idly, but demanded my full attention. Not only was it an exceptional piece of baking handiwork, but so much was going on with each bite that I had to find a quiet corner to fully focus on the pleasure of it.

Just as I was savoring a last bit of anise seed, Yoel, our guide, began to assemble his charges, about a dozen earnest parents, a jumble of pre-school children and me. A trim and grey sixty-something kibbutznik, Yoel informed us that this morning, we would experience how wheat had been harvested during the days of the Bible.

And so we set off, a straggling flock of Israelites following Yoel on the short walk to the kibbutz wheat field. Collecting ourselves next to a dusty row of dry wheat, we watched as Yoel reached down and pulled up a stalk by its roots, giving it a sharp kick with his foot to dislodge the clumps of dirt. "This is one way of harvesting wheat", he explained, "but not the only one." At that point, he handed out wooden-handled sickles and the parents hovered anxiously over their children as they took the curved blades and sawed away at the woody stalks. It was an hour till noon and the sun was beating hard on our backs as we stooped down to gather our harvest, pile it onto a large white sheet, gather up the edges and carry the bundle back to the threshing floor.

Wheat and barley, Yoel told us, are two of what are known as the "seven species" (Deuteronomy 8:8), the seven foods of the Promised Land that offered relief after forty years of a less-than-satisfactory desert diet. The fact that these two grains appear first and second on the list, according to our guide, indicated their pre-eminent place in the agriculture of the ancient Near East.

"Imagine," Yoel told us, "that you have worked hard since the winter and your crop of wheat is waist high and has already begun to produce its spikelets. At that point, if there isn't one good rain to give the plants that extra burst of energy to produce and fill out the seeds inside the hulls, they can reach maturity completely empty, without yielding any grain. What that simple, natural disaster signified was a year of famine for an entire community.

"Because the ancient Israelites were a farming people, the imperative to faithfully worship one god was easier to drive home if it was expressed in the terms that were closest to their hearts: *'If, then, you obey the commandments that I enjoin upon you this day, loving the Lord your God and serving Him with all your heart and soul, I will grant the rain for your land in season, the early rain and the late. You shall gather in your new grain and wine and oil.'* (Deuteronomy 11:13-14)

"But just to be on the safe side," Yoel whispered to me as an aside, "the farmer would bury a few fertility statues, borrowed from the Canaanite neighbors, in the earth as well."

Back at the museum, we spread the stalks of wheat out on the corner of the museum courtyard that was designated as the threshing floor. The children, assuming the roles of bulls and mules, shuffled over the stalks of wheat in the first step of the threshing process. After that, they yoked themselves in pairs to a wooden threshing sledge, identical to the one I'd seen at the museum in Sakhnin, to finish the job. We all took turns wielding the wooden pitchfork, tossing the threshed wheat into the air with a little shake so the grains fell straight downward and the chaff blew off to another pile. Then, on our hands and knees, we gathered up the kernels of grain and carried them to the milling corner. The kids settled around four different sets of grindstones for a brief dalliance with the time-consuming and back-breaking labor of grinding wheat into flour.

After a few minutes, their attention spent, the children exchanged the tickets they'd received with their entrance fee for a lump of dough, which they patted into shape, then baked on an outdoor oven in yet another corner of the courtyard. I gave my ticket to one of the children, not wanting to disturb the lingering memory of my *hubs al kaleb*, and wondered if children these days are even aware that flour is a product of wheat—and how many museum visitors realize that you don't need to look back thousands of years to see grindstones in action.

Ramadan in Nazareth

A handmill or an upper millstone shall not be taken in pawn, for that would be taking someone's life in pawn. Deuteronomy 24:6

I sent the photos to Balkees, explaining my interest in local culinary traditions, and we agreed that we should meet one day in Nazareth, the city where she lives. A few weeks later, she sent another mail, inviting my husband and me to join her family for dinner at their home. This was during the month of Ramadan, when observant Muslims fast between an early morning meal and the break-fast dinner known as *f'tur.* "Of course we would be pleased to come," I replied.

That evening, as twilight approached, we wound our way through the narrow streets of this densely-built-up Muslim and Christian city, and climbed a steep hill to reach Balkees's home— the top apartment in a three-story building entirely occupied by immediate family members. She welcomed us at the front door, then disappeared into the kitchen while we joined her husband Muhammad, an importer of building materials and descendant of a veteran Nazareth family, out on the balcony. In the golden evening light, we looked down at the fruit-laden fig and olive trees in the yard below, savoring the summer breeze and waiting for the call of the muezzin to announce the end of that day's fast.

It wasn't long before Balkees and her youngest daughter emerged from the kitchen, placing dish after dish on the long table, festively set for the parents, four children and two guests. According to tradition, we broke the fast with soup—a savory, rich vegetable *shoraba*. Then we turned to platters of the green-golden roasted wheat known as *freekeh,* topped with chicken blackened with pepper and allspice, rolls of thin, Druze-style pita wrapped around shredded spiced chicken and vegetables, stuffed baby eggplants and pale-green, pear-shaped squash, stuffed grape leaves and baby zucchini, and of course, a fresh stack of *hubs el kaleb.*

After dinner, the children went off to their rooms, leaving the four of us to enjoy our home-made *katayef,* the traditional Ramadan dessert of syrup-soaked pancakes folded over a chopped walnut and cinnamon mixture. Balkees explained that she sells her home-made cookies and cakes to neighbors and friends who appreciate their quality and artistry. She showed me on the screen of her cell phone an image of rows and rows of meticulously crimped ring-shaped date cookies she'd just prepared for a customer for the holiday.

She grew up, Balkees told us, in a family of *fellaheen* in the nearby village of Kfar Reine, where she still has family and friends, although only a few still practice agriculture. Using the grain they supply, she makes many of the wheat products she uses in her home. Every month or so, Muhammad takes a sack of wheat to a mill in the nearby town of Tamra to stock the house with fresh whole wheat flour. They buy *freekeh* from friends who produce it; to show us how it was ground, he motioned us to follow him out to the stairwell. On one of the steps sat a set of basalt grindstones the size of a platter, identical to what we'd used at the archaeological museum's wheat harvest day. "This has been in our family for generations," he explained, "and I just finished grinding the *freekeh* before you came." The following year, when the season for roasting green wheat came around, he promised they would take me to see how it is done.

Her family's land holdings were much larger when she was a child, Balkees explained, but then the choicest plots were appropriated by the Israeli government to build one of the neighborhoods of Upper Nazareth, and the compensation they received in no way offset the suffering over their loss. The painful memory filled the room and settled in the pit of my stomach. Out of a conversation that started over bread, four almost strangers sitting in a Nazareth living room were delicately treading on an aching scar of the conflict between Israeli Arabs and Jews. None of us could fix it, or make it go away. But it was the simple act of speaking and listening with open hearts that guided us through. That, and another serving of *katayef.*

Balkees and I

Since that Ramadan dinner, my friendship with Balkees has blossomed and deepened, creating for both of us a warm and cherished middle ground where our two widely divergent worlds meet. Balkees is ten years younger than I. She is a devout Muslim, yet like many modern urban women, she and her daughters wear pants and do not cover their heads. I am a secular Jew, fascinated by the scriptural texts for what they reveal about this land and how people once lived on it. She is my guide into that world.

Balkees is a mother fiercely devoted to her four children—two sons and two daughters—the youngest three in high school and the eldest daughter about to enter college. All her children have attended Catholic school, out of their parents' determination to give them the best education the city can offer. My two children went through the public school system; the eldest has completed military service and the youngest is about to start. Balkees's children's approach to the country's military, which does not invite them to join it, is much more ambivalent.

At the beginning of my friendship with Balkees, when we wanted to plan an outing together, she would insist that we return in time to serve her kids lunch when they came home from school. She loved getting out of the house, but the idea of not sitting with her children around the lunch table was inconceivable. Over time, she has become more flexible, and we are able to spend full days beyond the immediate Nazareth radius. But come two o'clock, I notice she grows quiet and pensive.

Balkees and I both work hard to communicate in Hebrew, approaching the language from opposite points on the compass. Her world view informs the words she chooses, and sometimes the imagery she uses is delightful. The people in Nazareth, she explains, can be like owls, meaning that they walk around grouchy and scowling. One of her worst insults, saved for big talkers who don't deliver the goods, is to be likened to a frog—"who doesn't lay eggs and doesn't produce milk—just goes kwak kwak." What about other animals, I asked her. "Well", she replied. "A cat is someone who rubs up against you all the time and just wants to be fed. And a dog is just a dog."

Returning Balkees's hospitality has proven to be a challenge. The first time I invited her family for dinner at our home, as soon as they walked in the door, I could see the look of horror on her face when she saw my cats sleeping on the furniture. After agonizing over the menu, I had decided to make lasagna, a dish she had told me that her children liked. I prepared my favorite spinach lasagna with goat cheese, a big mistake. This was not the lasagna the kids were familiar with, and they picked around the noodles. Balkees put a teaspoon-sized serving on her plate and didn't touch it. Only Muhammad ate with gusto, and with great compliments to the cook.

The next time I invited them for an outdoor barbeque. That was more successful. But I've since learned not to be offended by

Balkees's reticence over eating at my home, simply because she is like that almost anywhere. As a matter of principle, she doesn't like to eat in restaurants or anywhere outside her own home, as the food will never be as good as what she prepares, and the kitchen is undoubtedly not as clean as hers. And to a large extent, I'm inclined to believe she is right.

Kfar Reine

Balkees was raised on the wheat, vegetables, fruits and olive oil that were produced from the land around her, and they continue to define her culinary world. In long conversations, meals and excursions, I am learning how these foods shaped her childhood world and how she approaches them as a mature and gifted cook. With great pride and joy, she shares her knowledge and experiences with me.

One afternoon she took me and her girls to Kfar Reine to visit her uncle who still cultivates a small plot of land behind his house. The village abuts the hills of Nazareth, and her uncle's land sits in a deep ravine, with the newly-built homes of the expanding village looking down on all sides. As a child, Balkees was a frequent visitor in this home, but since she married and had a family, she comes here only infrequently, even though the distance separating their two homes is only a ten-minute drive. But it was a beautiful winter afternoon and the visit put her in high spirits.

We parked the car in the driveway and she skipped down to the field below, where her uncle was working—a lone figure in a patterned *keffiye*, wielding a scythe in the long grass. After warm greetings and introductions, Balkees explained to her uncle that we had come to see the wheat. "But there's no wheat this year," he explained. Now that the neighborhood is so developed, the combine could no longer make its way down to his field, so he was growing oats for animal feed instead. But that didn't matter to us.

Balkees led me down to an old well at the bottom of the property, housed in a crumbling concrete structure, perhaps built by the Germans sometime in the last century. Next to it, a small stream trickled by, almost hidden by the tall grass, and we gathered cress, called *jarjir ha nahal,* which grows wild next to water. To that we added an armful of *ellet,* and the girls picked green almonds from a tree to snack on. The air was cool and fragrant and we reveled in the greenery. Then we went into the house to see Balkees's aunt and cousins.

Wherever I go with Balkees, she lights up a room like a shooting star. When we visit her mother's home in Kfar Reine, within minutes a collection of siblings, nieces and nephews appear, and everyone gathers around to bask in her charm. And so it was here too: many kisses and hugs from the small group of women, as well as warm greetings for me, their welcome guest. They had just made a fresh batch of *tabouleh* and we each were served a plate piled high with the shiny green mixture, pungent from the parsley and lemons grown in their garden, delicately balanced with bulgur made from wheat grown in the village. While the conversation swirled around me, I sat back and enjoyed being in the company of these down-to-earth, rural women. Balkees told them funny stories and they bent over laughing; I watched their great affection for her and I was filled with it as well.

Tabouleh

Mix 1 large bunch of finely chopped parsley, 1 small bunch of finely chopped fresh mint, 2 chopped green onions, both the white and green parts, 1/4 cup finely ground bulgur, 3 Tbsp olive oil, lemon juice from about 3-4 large lemons, and salt to taste. Let the mixture sit until the juices soften the bulgur. For *Tabouleh* Salad, add finely chopped cucumbers, lettuce and/or tomatoes.

Maadele

For Balkees, cooking is an expression of her finest self. When I compliment her on yet another wonderful dish, she says "Everything I make is delicious." Muhammad brings home cartons of vegetables that he buys in the villages he passes during his work deliveries; she prepares the dishes she knows her family loves.

Where other women her age have abandoned the labor-intensive foods they grew up with, Balkees still spends mornings working her way through tall stacks of grape leaves, rolling them around a filling of rice or *freekeh* into cylinders as thin as cigarettes, finishing each one off with a tight squeeze before arranging them like sardines inside a pot, to cook wedged between stuffed baby zucchinis, under a layer of tomato slices. Other days she prepares *shishbarak*, rolling out thin layers of dough on the dining room table, and with a plastic soda bottle cap, cutting out dozens and dozens of tiny circles, each one of which she fills with a dab of seasoned ground meat and twists with a flourish into a perfect rosette. These little morsels will be simmered in yoghurt sauce, a hearty Arab rendition of tortellini.

I love watching Balkees prepare *mughrabiye*, the local version of couscous. Like a conductor whose orchestra is on the table underneath her, she rubs bulgur with grand sweeping motions across a broad platter, covering each grain with layer after layer of moistened flour. The coated grains are slowly steamed over a pot of rich chicken broth, and then served in a bowl with the chicken and the soup on top. Whatever she prepares, when the cooking is finished, she fixes a plate and sends one of the children to bring it downstairs to her in-laws.

And of course she makes her own *leben* and *labaneh* from sheep and goat milk that is delivered to her house once a week, and her own pickled peppers, cauliflowers and tiny eggplants. Most intriguing is Balkees's candied pumpkin. The first time I tried it, I was utterly at a loss to guess the origins of this shiny, orange sweet with a distinct crunchy bite that released a syrupy core. Even more bizarre was the method used to make it. The pieces of pumpkin are first soaked in water that has separated from whitewash, so that the lime gives it its distinctive texture. Then they are rinsed and soaked in syrup flavored with lemon geranium.

In between all the family meals, Balkees juggles the baking for her customers, who shower her with orders during wedding season, the month of Ramadan and the holidays that follow. Her specialties are *karakish*, a paper-thin, whole-wheat cracker mixed with sesame, nigella and anise seeds, *kaak ma ahjway*, ring-shaped cookies filled with dates (she buys the best quality whole dates and grinds them in a meat grinder), and a pale, buttery cookie called *ghraibe*, filled with ground pistachio or Turkish delight. She bakes in a special gas oven that Muhammad brought from Hebron, expertly sliding the baking sheets under or away from the flame. Sometimes I'll try and help her as she turns out row after row of cookies, but I can't approach her dexterity in working with the dough.

The mixture and balance of flavors intrigue Balkees and whenever she tries a new food, she immediately thinks how to improve it. One day Ron promised to teach her how to make American-style bagels. After watching him in our kitchen, the next day she called me, proud to report that she'd prepared her own version, with *zaatar* and nigella seeds. She invited us over and served them warm from the oven, spread with her home-made *labaneh*. She's a genius, I realized. Balkees had just invented the perfect centerpiece for a Jewish and Arab brunch!

· · ·

With time, Balkees began to let me help her in the kitchen, doing the menial tasks she could trust me with. One evening, as we prepared dinner, she handed me a huge bunch of parsley to clean. This meant separating the inferior, yellowing pieces from the nice green ones, into two piles. Each stalk of parsley, piece by piece, had to be examined—something I saw that I didn't have the patience to do. But I did my best, and when I finished, she gave a cursory look at the two piles and mumbled, "*Inti mish maadale.*" The "you aren't" part I understood. But what was *maadale? Maadale*, Balkees explained, describes someone who is both skillful and thrifty. Who doesn't throw away the good parsley with the bad.

Then she put me in front of a bowl of lemons and the electric juicer. When I'd finished and was about to throw the pulp away, again I heard, "*Inti mish maadale.*" She took the pulp, forced it through a sieve with the back of a spoon, and collected another quarter cup of juice. She put the juice in a jar with a few tablespoons of sugar, put the top on, and handed it to me. "Shake it up until the sugar dissolves." I shook for about ten seconds and thought, can I stop now? But it took longer for the sugar to dissolve, and I realized how my internal clock is wired for instant results. Now, Balkees was asking me to slow down. To pay attention to what I was doing. To give these foods the attention they deserve.

Sometimes I find myself telling Balkees to slow down as well. When she complains how harried she is, with seven different things to prepare, I suggest that she take a break, make a list and see if anything can be crossed off or postponed until later. "You don't always have to be a superwoman," I remind her.

Freekeh

*Ruth the Moabite said to Naomi, "I would like to go
to the fields and glean among the ears of grain,
behind someone who may show me kindness."* Ruth 2:2

Muhammad had promised that when the season came to make
freekeh, he would let us know. One spring morning, on a day when
Easter Monday and the last day of Passover coincided, Balkees called
to let us know that it was time. The normally congested roads into
Nazareth were empty because of the holidays, and within twenty
minutes Ron and I pulled up to Balkees's house. Soon the three of us
were heading out of the city, past the outlying villages and towards
the farmland belonging to her long-time family friend, Abu S. Very
few *fellaheen* in the Galilee still roast green wheat to produce *freekeh*
and we were excited and grateful that Abu S's sons, who do most of
the work, had agreed to let us join them in this task.

We turned onto a dirt road which led to Abu S's wheat fields.
There we were joined by the two younger sons, Falekh and Samekh,
lean and powerful young men in their early twenties. We noticed
that the field was divided unevenly; a small section of the crop was
green and the rest was already turning golden. The wheat in both

sections was partially ripe, the kernels fully formed and nutrition-
ally mature. But the golden wheat would be left to dry completely
on the stalk for at least another month before eventually being harvested by a combine, which would automatically separate the grain
from the ears as it worked. When making *freekeh*, however, the entire ear of the green wheat needed to be harvested intact, and for
that, machines were neither economical nor practical, leaving Abu
S's sons to do the job by hand.

Falekh passed each of us a wooden-handled sickle and demon-
strated how to wrap the blade around a bunch of wheat stalks just
below the ears, grab the tops with your left hand and then pull hard
toward you with the sickle in your right. Again, I was reminded of
the wheat day at the museum, although now, this Biblical labor was
being done for real, right here in the 21st century. With my sickle in
hand and up to my hips in wheat, I felt just like Ruth the Moabite.
The blades must just have been sharpened because they cut easily
through the brittle stalks. We tossed each handful of wheat tops into
a large canvas sack that we dragged along behind us as we worked.

In this unusually cool spring, the noontime sun wasn't oppressive and the work was pleasant and meditative. Balkees, Ron
and I progressed slowly through the field, while Falekh and Samekh
surged ahead. The image of cotton pickers came to mind. Knowing
that there are many traditional *fellah* work songs, I asked Falekh
if they ever sang while working. He dismissed my question with
a scowl, and I understood that this piece of old-time folklore had
fallen by the wayside, leaving only the hard work behind.

Balkees took an ear of the green wheat and peeled away a kernel to show me. It was the size of a grain of rice. Then she squeezed

it and a little drop of milky liquid was released. This, she explained, was the gluten, and the reason why this stage of ripeness is sometimes called the milk stage. We peeled more kernels out of the ear and popped them into our mouths. They were sweet and refreshing.

If you bring a meal offering of first fruits to the Lord, you shall
bring new ears parched with fire, grits of the fresh grain,
as your meal offering of first fruits. Leviticus 2:14

Any awareness of the various stages in the growing cycle of grain has largely disappeared from our general consciousness. The Bible, however, uses specific terms for grain in different stages of ripeness. "*Aviv*", the modern Hebrew word for "spring", refers in the Bible to grain that is still green, though its kernels are almost fully ripe within the ears. "*Carmel*" signifies a slightly later stage of ripeness, but before the ear has fully dried and turned golden. Dr. Tova Dickstein, an expert in Biblical foods at the Neot Kedumim Biblical Landscape Reserve, explains that, during the eighth plague in the Exodus narrative, hailstones destroyed the Egyptian barley crop because it was *aviv*, implying that the stalks were hollow and brittle, as opposed to the slower ripening wheat and flax, whose stalks were still green and supple. In Leviticus 2:14, the new ears in the original Hebrew text are literally *aviv*, and the fresh grain, *carmel*.

•   •   •

After about an hour in the field, the eldest brother drove up on a tractor, signaling that we were to move on to the next stage of work. He loaded the two sacks we had managed to fill onto a wagon, and we followed the tractor up a low hill to the threshing floor. At the periphery of this flattened expanse, large tarps had been spread on which ears of wheat were already drying in the sun—some just picked and others already charred and black after having been roasted in the fire.

An old metal bed frame stood in the middle of the threshing floor, with a sheet of thick wire mesh balanced on top of it. Onto this the brothers were piling armloads of the dry green ears of wheat. One of them ignited the pile on either end with a cigarette lighter, turning the packed wheat over with a pitchfork to spread the flames. The object is to char the outer hull which makes it easier to thresh away the chaff, while roasting the inside kernel of grain. The moisture in the grain keeps it from burning, but it does take on a distinctive smoky flavor. In the past, the wheat used to be roasted on a bed of barley stalks—the barley and *freekeh* harvests more or less coincide—and the dry stalks provided excellent fuel. Today, when the pile doesn't ignite well enough, a blow torch attached to a tank of butane gas speeds up the process.

Once they were blackened, the heads of wheat were spread in a thin layer on a tarp to dry in the sun. The brothers continued burning more wheat, a hot, dirty and back-breaking process which would go on for several days. When all the roasted wheat was sufficiently dry, a tractor-operated threshing machine would come to the farm, making its rounds among the *freekeh* producers in the Galilee. Once the grains were separated from the chaff and cleaned, they would be stored away, this time in the shade to prevent the sun from bleaching away their distinctive green color. Finally, the dried *freekeh* would be taken to a mill in one of the nearby Arab villages for grinding—coarse for regular cooking and fine for use when making *freekeh* soup.

Balkees picked up one of the blackened heads of wheat and rubbed it between her hands, then opened them and puffed. The chaff blew away in the breeze, leaving half a dozen shiny green grains resting on her palms. "Repeat after me," she said. *"Eshna udukna kher esini.* This is the blessing we say when we taste the first fruit of a new season," she explained. I remembered the *shehechiyanu* Jewish prayer, recited for the same purpose. After that, we tasted a few kernels, savoring the grassy, smoky, chewy moment.

. . .

The word *freekeh* relates to the Arabic and Hebrew verbs for separate or rub apart, describing the hand motion used to separate the roasted grain from the chaff. In her research of scriptural translations, Dr. Dickstein discovered in the Aramaic *Onkelos* translation of the Bible, the Hebrew word *carmel* became *firokhan* in Aramaic.

Coarsely ground *freekeh* looks like shiny greenish bulgur and is cooked in a similar fashion. I like the version I learned from my friend Nuzha, prepared like pilaf with browned vermicelli shards, where the smoky rich flavor somehow reminds me of Rice-a-Roni. Balkees disapproves of this version. *Freekeh* stands alone, she explains, and should not be mixed with anything else. To drive that point home, she recites a saying: *Ana mithal freekeh—baqbalish sharike.* Roughly translated, this means, I'm like *freekeh*; I don't like partners, and can be understood as being said by a woman who does not want to share her husband with any other spouse. At home, Balkees prepares *freekeh* out of the broth in which she cooks a richly seasoned chicken, serving the greenish gold grain as a side dish. Her *freekeh* soup is fragrant with the smoky flavor of the grains, which settle lightly at the bottom of the bowl.

Freekeh can be bought here in most Arab stores and markets, but it is often imported from Jordan or Turkey. Abu S can't compete with these cheap imports, but there are still those who prefer to acquire the superior, fresh local product directly from the source. For that, they must make the trip to the family home in the village adjacent to the fields.

A few weeks after our harvest day, Balkees and I headed to Abu S's home to buy some fresh *freekeh*. Um S welcomed us outside, next to the yard where she keeps goats, sheep and chickens. A tall, broad-shouldered woman in traditional village dress, she led the way to the basement where the fresh roasted grain—whole and milled—lay piled on canvas sheets spread on the floor.

Abraham hastened into the tent to Sarah,
and said, "Quick, three seahs of choice flour!" Genesis 18:6

I asked for a kilo of the coarsely ground *freekeh*, and Um S measured it out for me on a digital scale. I noticed a large empty metal can about the size of an institutional pickle container resting on one of the mounds of grain. From memories of the museum in Sakhnin, I suspected that I knew what it was. Um S confirmed that it was a *seah*, the nominal measure of grain cited in the Bible, its present calibration approximating six kilos. And here it was, outside a museum, still being used! For Um S, the *seah* was simply a standard and convenient measure acceptable to her customers.

How many people, I wondered, after thousands of years and in our metric day and age, could still be measuring their grain by the *seah*? A few days later I asked Abu Malek about the *seah*. "Oh, that hasn't been used since the 1940s," he replied. But then Um Malek corrected him. "No, they still use it around Nazareth," she explained. But probably not for much longer.

Um S would not accept money for the kilo of fresh *freekeh* I took, acknowledging my small contribution to the *freekeh*-making process. But I did manage to purchase a bucket of fresh, thick goat milk *leben* and several slabs of her home-made, salty goat milk cheese known as *jibni*. As one of her daughters went to wrap up the cheese, Um S, Balkees and I sat in her living room, drinking tiny cups of black coffee. While they chatted, I was delighted to find how many words and phrases I could now recognize.

Their family, Um S told us, is the last one left in their village that still lives entirely from agriculture. I know from Balkees that the sons would prefer a less demanding and more lucrative occupation than farming. But in the meantime, preparations for the crops of vegetables must be attended to even before the *freekeh* harvest is over, and there is no respite from their toil. We left with Balkees's parting blessing to Um S, *ya tiku el affiyeh*: May you have the strength to carry on—and I added a silent Amen.

Freekeh (with partners)

For 4 servings. Wash 1 1/2 cups of coarsely ground *freekeh* in several changes of water. Crumble a handful of thin spaghetti and brown for a minute or two in hot olive oil in a small pot with a lid, stirring constantly. Add the drained *freekeh* and stir well. Add 3 cups of broth, a half teaspoon of *baharat* spice mixture and salt and pepper to taste. Bring to a boil, lower heat and cover. Cook until all the liquid is absorbed and the *freekeh* is soft—about 15 minutes. Serve garnished with toasted pine nuts and slivered almonds.

Nazareth

My first image of Nazareth, formed in a long-ago art history class, featured a placid, indigo-robed Mary and a lavishly winged angel murmuring secrets in a pristine, geometrically tiled room. These days, it's difficult to reconcile that image with the humming, Middle Eastern city I so often visit. Difficult, but not impossible.

Nazareth is a short twenty-minute drive and a world away from my Jezreel Valley home. Built into a deep topographic bowl, it is Israel's largest Arab city, where some 75 thousand Muslim and Christian residents share some of the most densely populated urban space in the country.

The historic core of the city radiates out from the Grotto of the Annunciation and Mary's Well, with the old city market and commercial and residential areas extending upwards along the sloping hillsides. On the western ridge, a golden dome and minaret, basilicas and apartment buildings vie for dominance over the skyline. Mount Precipice, with its massive carved amphitheater, is further south, its view of Mount Tabor obstructed by urban hills. To the east are the shopping centers and high-rise apartment buildings of Upper Nazareth, a predominantly Jewish city established by the Israeli government in the late 1950s in an official attempt to create demographic counterweight. By and large, the upper and lower cities turn a cold shoulder one to the other.

My route to Nazareth approaches the city from the west, passing farmlands, forest, and Jewish and Bedouin rural villages before ascending abruptly into an urban sprawl of sand-colored buildings. Yaffia was originally its own discreet village, separated from Nazareth by a hill and a deep valley. But when motor vehicles and paved roads redefined notions of distance, Yaffia was quietly subsumed to the status of a Nazareth suburb.

Yaffia's main thoroughfare is lined with garages and auto parts shops, lamp and toy stores, fruit and vegetable markets and clothing stores, their wares spilling out beyond the confines of the storefronts. Dusty palm trees stand rank and file along the median strip. Suspended from the street lights and telephone poles, strings of holiday lights hang limp and lusterless, waiting for the nights of the Christmas season and month of Ramadan to shine. Across signboards and on the street, the *lingua franca* shifts from Hebrew to Arabic.

When I first began coming to Nazareth, every time I entered the city felt like crossing into a foreign country. There was that familiar frisson of tension that comes before facing an unfamiliar culture and language. Would I be treated graciously or with hostility as a foreigner, a woman and a Jew?

I no longer experience those feelings. I've spent enough time in Nazareth to be oriented and comfortable. And I've learned to approach the people I meet as a guest in their city, with courtesy, a smile and an open heart. Repeated often enough, these gestures of friendship are usually returned in kind. After countless trips through the old city market, the returns on my investment in trust-building are inestimable.

I leave my car near Paulus VIth Street, Nazareth's congested main drag, and make my way by foot towards the market, crossing a large paved plaza emblazoned with banners quoting from the Koran in Arabic and English. Not so long ago, an ill-fated plan to build a mosque on this plaza, just steps away from the city's main church and in advance of a long-anticipated Millennium visit by the Pope, set off an explosion of violence between the Muslim and Christian communities. The plan was eventually shelved, and only the banners remain.

I come to Nazareth for an immersion course in local seasonal foods, and the intriguing, narrow, stone-paved passageways of the Ottoman-era market are my classroom. The market greets its visitors in thematic stages. It opens up just above the main plaza, under the shadow of the monumental modern church that encompasses the Grotto of the Annunciation. Here, on either side of the street, are the souvenir shops, crowded with olive wood statuettes, blue glass evil eye amulets and vials of holy water. One of these shops belongs to the Taha family, whose patriarch, Taha Muhammad Ali was a celebrated Palestinian poet. I often saw him seated at the entrance to his store, watching the tourists go by, and fortunately, was able to tell him how his poetry touched me before he died.

Continuing up the steep, stone-paved road, past the Church of the Annunciation and through a stone archway, the main walkway suddenly narrows down into a shoulder-to- shoulder, two-pedestrian lane tunnel, where the market really begins. Racks of T-shirts, women's robes and housewares press in on all sides. Heavy gold chains and rings flash in shop displays. A smiling shoemaker in a red fez works on the heel of a boot, entirely filling the nook his shop has carved out of the old stone wall. Shoppers heading upstream make way for those on their way down. From a CD vendor's speakers, aching songs of love and loss sung by Lebanese superstars float through the air, a reminder that in this part of the world, the cultural center of gravity pulls to the east.

A sharp turn in the maze of passageways marks the unofficial entrance to the vegetable market. In the cool shadows of a vaulted stone archway, I know I'll find the same vendor whose repertoire of wares shifts from stacks of grape leaves, crates of okra and long green pods of black-eyed peas in the summer to bunches of *ellet*, *zaatar* and *selek* in the winter. After a few more steps, the narrow covered passage opens into the produce market's main plaza.

• • •

Up until a few decades ago, when most Arab villages had only the most rudimentary stores to serve them, Nazareth was the Galilee's commercial and cultural metropolis, and a trip to the Nazareth market entailed all the excitement of a big-city shopping expedition. It was the place to purchase coffee, sugar and other items that couldn't be raised or made on one's own. And it was a watering hole at which to meet more distant villagers and catch up on local news.

Before the Christian and Muslim holidays, whole families came to Nazareth to outfit themselves in new clothing and shoes. For couples about to be married, the quarter known as the bride's market was the destination to purchase wedding clothes, supplies and gold jewelry for the celebration, and linens and household goods for their future home.

In shops along the alleyways, metal workers repaired agricultural equipment, carpenters built furniture, and a local potter sold kitchenware fashioned from clay dug out of a Nazareth hillside. During the wheat harvest season, villagers loaded their donkeys with sacks of grain to be milled at the El Babour Mill, one of the first steam engine-driven mills in the Galilee, originally established by German Templers. For their part, the villagers brought in their own produce and animals to sell to the urbanites.

After the war of 1948, Nazareth absorbed a massive influx of refugees, mainly Muslim Palestinian *fellaheen* bereft of their villages, homes and land. With their livelihood swept out from underneath them, and the wheat-centered economy only a memory, many *fellaheen* in Nazareth and across the Galilee became laborers, building the cities, roads and homes of modern Israel. No longer producing their own food, they began spending their salaries in the stores and shopping centers that cropped up at the city's periphery and in every town and village. In the Nazareth market, with the traditional flow of customers diverted, many of the merchants either closed up shop or shifted their focus to tourism.

But tourists are averse to political unrest. Just as tensions over the planned mosque were subsiding, the Second Intifada broke out in October 2000. This time the violence and rage that erupted in the streets of Nazareth paralyzed the city and deepened the chasm between Arabs and Jews for years to come. Local and foreign visitors shunned the city, the market closed in on itself, and petty criminals roamed the abandoned alleyways. Over a decade later, and ever so slowly, the market is now coming back to life, and busloads of pilgrims from India, Russia and Europe are a welcome sight.

Market Season

Beyond the pedestrian fruits and vegetables on display, I'm always on the lookout for the local seasonal specialties that are virtually unknown outside the Arab market. Mainly, they are gathered from the wild or come from the small local farms of *fellaheen* that cater to Arab clientele.

In the summer, there are sacks of green almonds, their soft fuzzy shells pliable enough to crack open between your teeth in order to reach the sweet, bleached kernel inside. Crates of pale green bottle squash remind me of their name in Arabic, *kareh'ah*, which is so challenging for me to pronounce. These, along with zucchini no longer than my finger and miniature eggplants the size of an egg, are hollowed out and stuffed with a mixture of rice and chopped meat, then cooked in tomato sauce. Stuffed vegetables, stuffed grape leaves, okra and the fresh whole pods of black eyed peas are all standard summer fare I've savored at Balkees's table and in Arab homes across the Galilee.

There are green figs and purple ones in as many varieties as the microclimates they grow in. There are tiny, yellow-red, intensely flavorful apricots whose season is as short as a breath, ending when they succumb to the worms that wait just as eagerly for them to ripen. Piles of *sabras*, the fruit of the cactus plant, tempt those willing to contend with their spiny outer skin and a mouthful of seeds.

In the autumn, for those who don't have access to their own

trees, vendors sell freshly-picked Suri olives. Conveniently set up next to the olive vendors, an old-time, olive-cracking machine will save you the job of knocking each fruit with a stone so the salty brine can permeate its skin.

Come winter, I know there is one special corner of the market where a small group of Bedouin women spread out the edible wild plants they gather—*hubeisa*, *ellet* and *selek*, *elsaina* and wild asparagus. Squatting on the ground behind their display of greens, they coyly offer fresh eggs in small baskets full of straw and containers of home-made *jibni*, half concealed by the folds of their robes.

The first appearance of vine leaves and the soft-skinned squashes are signs of a shift into spring, and they bear the prohibitive price tags of haute cuisine. But in the market's spring fresh-food fest, the short green chickpea season is a highlight. The entire chickpea plant is sold, roots and all, each stalk adorned with some half-dozen pods dangling like sleigh bells. People walk through the market, stalks in hand, plucking off the pods and cracking the pliant shell to munch on the soft, bright green, and perfectly formed chick pea inside—the perfect spring snack food.

By late afternoon, the vendors pack up their stalls and street sweepers collect the discarded cabbage leaves and crushed fruit. Around the plaza, private palaces built in the 19th century by wealthy landowning families look down onto the street below from triple arched windows high up on the second floor. The Venetian-inspired architecture, imported by traders familiar with the Italian port, exudes European grace, even as so many of these homes stand neglected or empty.

. . .

Balkees's husband once had a clothing store in the market, which has been closed and shuttered for almost twenty years. But when she and I walk through the market, Muhammad's old friends still greet her like neighbors. There is an elderly gentleman, one of the last of the local craftsmen still producing hand-made knives, whose tiny jumbled workspace is directly across from the site of Muhammad's former store. Bending over his anvil, he keeps his back turned to deflect inquisitive passersby, but is always pleased to see Balkees. Whenever an idea for a better baking tool comes to mind, she likes to consult with him about it.

As a source for the freshest spices, Balkees prefers the *Fahoum* coffee store. The red-smocked proprietor roasts green coffee beans in a massive, ancient machine in the back room of his vaulted-ceilinged shop, then grinds them and mixes the fragrant lot in a giant round aluminum tray, adding great swirling scoopfuls of pale ground cardamom. Trim and formal, with cropped red hair and thick glasses, he weighs out sumac, pepper, allspice and *baharat* mixture from glass jars for Balkees, and his stout, smiling assistant serves us small cups of *saada*. Balkees is certain he keeps the notebook with the formula for mixing his own *baharat*, inherited from his father, in a safe.

Genial and portly Abu Ashraf welcomes tourists and locals in four languages to his grotto of a restaurant in the vegetable market. Wearing a white apron to cover his ample middle, he pours batter out of a galvanized metal watering-can-like dispenser onto a hot griddle to make *katayif*. These little pancakes are traditionally eaten only during Ramadan, but Abu Ashraf serves them all year long, folded over a filling of chopped nuts and cinnamon or *jibni*, browned in oil and then drenched in syrup. He also sells just the pancakes, one of the very few culinary short-cuts I've ever seen Balkees indulge in.

El Babour, the former flour mill, has made the transition into modern times by transforming itself into an emporium for spices, grains and dry comestibles. I liken it to a magical treasure trove for foodies. A fragrant cloud greets us even before we step through the store's low doorway and onto the landing of a high set of stone stairs. I'm intoxicated by the cavernous vaulted space below, its floor and tables lined with opened sacks of every kind of dried leaf, seed or grain you can imagine, in hues of saffron, olive and sesame. A wooden threshing sledge and various old farming implements are affixed high up on the stone walls. A young saleswoman in a red El Babour shirt, with kohl-lined eyes and hair covered in a bright headscarf, greets us with a warm smile, ready to fill Balkees's order.

While she buys anise and nigella seeds for her baking, I make my way to my favorite part of the store, off limits to all but staff, which Tony, the owner has given me carte blanche access. Descending a short set of stairs, I pass through another massive vaulted storeroom, its walls painted warm orange and green. Piled sacks of grains and spices almost hide the old flour milling machinery, partially dismantled and virtually invisible in its obsolescence. The din that once filled this room, the procession of sacks emptied and filled, and the air thick with flour exist in Tony Kanaza's most vivid childhood memories. He remembers as a small boy the day he realized that his father's hair wasn't really white.

An open doorway spills light into the room and leads out to a small, walled courtyard. Here, when the flour mill was still operating, customers used to wait with their donkeys and bags of wheat for their turn at the mill. The courtyard is relatively small, and I imagine that only about five or six customers could wait there at one time. In the center, there is a stone well, now covered and dry, that once refreshed them as they bided their time.

Today, the courtyard is filled with a fascinating array of milling, roasting and other miscellaneous pieces of machinery. In one corner stands an olive cracking machine. Next to it is an oven for roasting sesame seeds. *Zaatar* leaves are spread on a tarp on the ground, drying in the open air. In a small mill, cumin seeds are being ground and their scent fills my entire head.

One lucky day I happened to be in the courtyard when an old couple from one of the villages arrived carrying a pillowcase full of *freekeh* to be milled. They handed their bundle to a young, red-shirted worker who fed the whole kernels of roasted green wheat into a small mechanical mill. He collected the ground grain in a pail and took it to the thresher. The mill was a compact, shiny blue-painted metal device, but the rough wooden thresher with its tall hopper looked like it was straight out of an old-time farm museum. Still, it worked on electricity and when the young man plugged one extension cord into another, the thresher started to whir. The finely milled *freekeh* poured out of one chute, the coarser grain from another, and the finest chaff spilled into a waste bucket from a third. The old man put his hand into the stream of chaff and examined it, anxious not to lose any precious grain. I watched this quiet scene unfold, a ritual worlds removed from supermarket aisles and shelves, and placed an imaginary frame around it.

The Inn

Discreet signs along the market's alleyways point the way to the Fauzi Azar Inn, a hostel for backpackers and budget travelers, and a relative newcomer to Nazareth's old city. The signs lead past the produce market and a bakery turning out fresh pita bread off a creaky conveyor belt, through narrow alleyways, and up to the Inn's small, green wooden door. Passing through that portal, like entering El Babour. takes you into another world. But instead of a riot of color, smells and commerce, the interior courtyard of the Fauzi Azar Inn is a tranquil, timeless, liminal space. Above high stone walls and arches, a patch of blue sky is visible, and in one corner, a carved stone drinking trough has been transformed into a small fountain. Potted geraniums splash green and scarlet against the warm golden stone.

Less than ten years ago, when Maoz Yinon, a young hiker and entrepreneur, entered this courtyard, it was ankle-high in garbage. Maoz was looking for a place to create a hostel along the lines of those he'd visited on hiking routes across Europe and South America. Behind the thick veil of neglect, Maoz could see that he was standing in front of a historic palace, with the classic triple-arched windows and painted ceilings inspired by Venetian palazzos.

Maoz succeeded in convincing the Christian Arab family that owned the property that his hostel would be a strong enough draw to attract visitors into the run-down and dangerous old city market. The final condition that sealed the partnership was that the hostel would bear the name of the family patriarch. In 1996, the Fauzi Azar Inn opened after a bare-bones restoration and with three guest rooms. These days, thanks to its funky Old World charm and glowing recommendations from *The Lonely Planet* guide, the inn attracts a steady stream of guests who hike, bike and bus into the city from just about everywhere, breathing new life into the city and the market.

A steep set of stairs with an ornate metal banister leads from the courtyard to the building's main floor. At the top is a doorway into the *diwan*, or main salon, which now serves as the reception area and informal lobby. Once again, stepping into this space is momentarily and exquisitely disorienting. The room is grand, light and airy, and in spite of its minimalistic restoration, the opulent black and white marble floors, soaring arched windows, elaborate chandelier and lofty, ornate frescoed ceiling are reminders that this is indeed a palace. An ornately-framed photo of Fauzi Azar is hung in a place of honor on one of the walls. Young people from Finland, Germany and China lounge on couches, reading their guidebooks.

Suraida, Fauzi Azar's distinguished granddaughter and manager of the inn, reigns over the reception area. From behind an antique wooden desk, she takes calls and converses with staff and guests, switching effortlessly from Arabic to English to Hebrew. Above our heads, the magnificent painted ceiling, sky blue with garlands of flowers, is no less stunning for lack of restoration, its colors, set down by an itinerant Lebanese artist in the 19th century, are faded but true. At either end of the ceiling, the artist painted a cherub, each one hugging a sheaf of wheat. Looking carefully, you can see that one angel's sheaf is bright yellow and the other's is deep green—a testament to the sanctity of wheat in the Galilee, and to the two harvest seasons—one for *freekeh* and one for flour.

I love to spend time on one of the couches in the *diwan*, bask-ing in the light that spills into this ethereal space, with its high arched windows and geometric tiled floor straight out of a Flemish painting, listening to the quiet murmurings in a world of languages. I know there is a profound message to be heard here, and it fills me with hope.

Growing *Baal*

By the sweat of your brow shall you get bread to eat... Genesis 3:19

It took weeks before Balkees could find a free afternoon for us to go visit Um S in her vegetable field. Summer is wedding season and she was under relentless pressure to fill customer's orders. Practically not a day went by without someone calling to ask for 5 kilos of *karakish*, or 200 date-filled cookies.

At Arab weddings, Balkees explained, an undercover competition is played out at the dessert buffet tables as hostesses vie to impress their guests with the exceptional quality and array of sweets. The recent revival of *karakish*—wafer-thin, whole wheat sweet crackers seasoned with anise and sesame—has made it the current, must-have wedding confection. Preparing *karakish* demands special expertise to handle and bake the paper-thin dough, which most home bakers don't have, and only a few select bakeries offer it, only by special order. Balkees's *karakish* are her own enhancement of her mother's recipe, and wedding guests frequently end up calling her to order them for their own celebrations. Faced with the challenge of impressing ever more discerning guests, hostesses seek the advantage of home-prepared creations. At this point, Balkees has earned the reputation of having the hands of an artist.

Sitting in her living room, I watched Balkees peel away layers of *karakish* dough from a pile on the dining room table. Earlier in the day, she had rolled out the dough until it was practically transparent, then separated the leaves between folds of a sheet. With a flourish, she flipped each sheet of dough onto a baking tray, then sliced it with a rolling cutter into rectangles the size of greeting cards. The tray went into her custom-built oven—a galvanized metal box on legs, with gas jets along the bottom and two outward-opening front doors, the closest thing I've seen to baking over an open fire on the 3rd floor of an apartment building. Balkees just wanted to finish this last batch to complete the order, before she could take off for the rest of the day.

Baking each tray of delicate *karakish* takes only a minute or two, and she expertly flipped the tray around so that every side baked evenly, with the oven doors open the entire time. A momentary distraction and the entire pan would be blackened and useless. I sat quietly, trying to be a help and not a nuisance, placing ring-shaped date cookies in paper cupcake liners.

All this labor-intensive and time-consuming baking had to be squeezed into Balkees's normal, demanding routine of maintaining the household and preparing fresh, hot meals for her family of six. During wedding season, it seemed that every time we spoke, Balkees complained that she was completely worn out. There would be no respite, however, even though the month of Ramadan[2] would soon bring the wedding season to a grinding halt. During that entire month the family would shift into a rhythm of daily fasting

---

[2]Set according to the lunar calendar, the month of Ramadan is inching forward by 11 days each year, and will fall during summer for some years to come.

---

from 4 a.m. until sunset. Yet despite the high summer heat and fatigue from fasting, a daily *"f'tur"* meal to break the fast would have to be prepared, and orders would continue to come in.

But Ramadan was still two weeks away, and this latest order was finally finished, packed into aluminum trays and waiting on the table to be picked up. Ron and Muhammad finished their coffee and we headed out the door and down to the street. The four of us piled into Muhammad's pick-up truck and headed out of the city towards Um S's field. After about ten minutes, we veered off the main highway. As we bounced along the unmarked dirt road, it occurred to me that this was like taking a trip back in time, leaving the comforts and convenience of our modern lives behind us on the asphalt.

As we pulled up in front of the field, I tried to get my bearings. This was the first time we'd been there since the previous summer, and everything had been moved around. Zucchini was growing where last year the tomatoes were laid out. The okra plants were in the zucchini's rows. And the *fakus*—those pale green, hairy cucumbers that are such a pleasure to bite into, straight from the vine— were scattered here and there among the rows, random treasures to be discovered by the harvester. As Balkees explained, for those *fellaheen* who still practice this type of traditional agriculture, crop rotation is one of the few tools in the arsenal for ensuring a bountiful crop, and it is surely one of the most ancient.

This parcel of land and others around it, tucked into the hills between Nazareth and Kfar Kana, are not served by the national water system. Yet they are still being farmed by local families as they have been for millennia, without any external watering. In Arabic and Hebrew, this is called *baal* agriculture. Balkees read to me from the Arabic dictionary that *baal* refers to plants grown with only the water from the sky.

For the land that you are about to enter and possess is not like the land of Egypt from which you have come. There the grain you sowed had to be watered by your own labors, like a vegetable garden; but the land you are about to cross into and possess, a land of hills and valleys, soaks up its water from the rains of heaven. Deuteronomy 11:10-11

The Promised Land is described in Deuteronomy 11:10-11 in agricultural terms, as a place where the water supply was not the Nile, but a celestial guarantee. Taking into account the hot, dry conditions of the Middle East, this is a wondrous promise indeed.

Yet, in fact, the topography and climate of the Lower Galilee is exactly synchronized for this type of farming. The winter rainfall is generally sufficient for raising crops of wheat and barley, and the land retains enough moisture to sustain a summer vegetable season, augmented by local springs if one is so fortunate, or just the dew that collects on the plants during the cool early mornings of summer. Balkees once showed me how the leaves on a local variety of zucchini plant are perfectly designed to collect the dew and deliver it down the stem toward the roots.

This is how the land was farmed here in the Galilee, with water from the sky and the earth, from the advent of organized agriculture some ten thousand years ago, more or less, until modern Israel's agricultural cooperatives ushered local farming into the 20th century. With innovations like drip irrigation, hybrid plant varieties, and greenhouse cultivation, the ancient and delicate balance between land, rain, plant and farmer was put aside—except in these few isolated fields.

. . .

Um S and her sons convene at the field in the late afternoon hours, when their daytime work is over and the mid-summer heat begins to dissipate. By the time we arrived, they were already scattered out among the rows, each with a pail, collecting the tomatoes, zucchini, bottle squash and okra that had ripened since the harvesting of the previous day.

Um S is a large woman—over six feet tall. From the top of her scarf-covered head to the hem of her floor-length robes, she stands as solid as a mountain. If one were ever temped to romanticize the life of the traditional farmer, one need only get to know Um S and her family to understand the relentless, backbreaking toil that it entails. The late afternoon shift in the vegetable field is just another station in the daily course of her labors, a series of tasks that includes feeding and milking the herd of sheep and goats, pasteurizing the milk and making *leben* and *jibni*, and maintaining a household, including cooking a daily hot meal for a family of nine. Abu S oversees a herd of beef cattle, his oldest son helping him full time, while the two younger brothers work at construction jobs and take on their duties at the family farm after a full day at the work site. The two eldest daughters are married, but the younger girls still live at home and help with the household chores. There is no point in training them for work in the fields as they will surely not marry farmers.

I have been visiting Um S and her family for several years now, and in spite of our almost total dependence on Balkees to translate, the affection between us is great, and we greeted each other warmly, with kisses on the cheeks and hands on our hearts; her sons, with modest handshakes. Balkees and I joined Falekh among the rows of low-growing okra plants. Picking okra is tricky; the flowers, rolled into themselves at that evening hour, suspiciously resembled the mature pods and I had to look carefully not to nip a potential pod in the bud.

The lyrics of a popular Israeli song apply very nicely to okra harvesting: what you can see from there can't be seen from here. In other words, a single okra plant needs to be approached from every angle in order to reveal the pods hiding among its leaves. Detaching them from the plant requires an assertive twist of the wrist. Falekh flipped off the okra pods and tossed them behind his back into the pail like a basketball pro.

Picking okra is one of my favorite tasks, in spite of the little fibers that make your hands and arms itch. I marvel at the unique size and shape of each pod, different as shells at the beach, and this makes me a very slow harvester.

Balkees practically stepped on a large chameleon that was trawling for insects among the okra plants, its green and grey splotches magically mimicking the surrounding soil. It maneuvered over the crumbly earth on comical two-digit feet, rolling its dome-shaped eyes at bizarre angles. We were relieved that the reptile life we encountered that afternoon was so benign; poisonous snakes are a common danger in the summer vegetable rows.

The okra rows finished, we joined Um S and Samekh in the tomatoes. Nestled among vines that hugged the ground, the fruit was splayed in a jumble of sizes, shapes and shades of green and red, so different from the orderly rows of a modern farm. The tomatoes twisted into themselves in bizarre folds, with dark rough spots that a fastidious shopper would summarily pass over. No neat, sandwich bread-sized slices would come from these specimens. They ripened unevenly, their skins blushing from pale lime to crimson. Many were rotting on the ground.

It was hard to know which ones should be picked, and I watched Um S and Samekh for guidance. As close as I could gather, they were targeting the large green tomatoes and the small red ones. The green tomatoes, Muhammad explained to us later, are for eating. Left on the counter, they will continue to ripen and develop their flavor. The red ones needed to be used at once for cooking. Balkees cuts them into pieces and puts them straight into the blender to make tomato puree. By the end of the season, her freezer will be lined with bags of it.

It takes a specific variety of tomato to thrive under *baal* conditions. Um S and her neighbors have been growing this variety season after season. At the end of every summer, she saves seeds from that year's crop. She stores them through the winter, Balkees told me, in ashes. One year, when her seed stockpile was accidentally ruined, her brother shared from his own supply.

Plant varieties that are saved from year to year, and which grow out in the open, without greenhouse protection, are often referred to as *baladi*. It is common in produce markets to encounter these heirloom vegetables—particularly eggplants—advertised as being *baladi*. Coming from the Arabic word for village, *baladi* resonates with the promise of long-lost flavor. The tomatoes we were harvesting were both *baal* and *baladi*, a treasure almost unheard of. Yet ironically, Um S's local customers pay no special premium for this exceptional produce.

The growing season for *baal* vegetables is only a few short months, and Um S's yields are only a fraction of what contemporary, irrigation-based agriculture can produce. But this is what they have, and this is what they know. So this is what they grow. And I suspect that, once a more profitable and less thankless option for making a living presents itself, this field will eventually lie fallow.

Just as the sun slid burnt orange behind the western hills, a pale and perfect full moon rose on the opposite end of the sky. The young men loaded the buckets of vegetables onto a beat-up old station wagon whose single duty is to ferry back and forth between the fields, the corral where Abu S keeps his cattle, and the nearby house. We followed behind, stopping at the corral to meet Abu S. This is his domain, with an old train carriage on blocks that serves as a storage space, and next to it, a grape-vine covered wooden pergola.

We joined him on plastic chairs set up under the leafy roof, looking out towards the threshing floor where the annual *freekeh*-roasting ritual takes place. Cups of black coffee were passed around and we chatted easily in the twilight. That year Abu S had planted a small plot of tobacco next to the train car, healthy-looking, broad-leaved plants that he would both harvest and roll into cigarettes for his own consumption. I figured that makes him a "smokavore."

We carried home a small sack of okra and two larger bags of tomatoes, one green and one red, exuding a fragrance of distilled summer spice. At home I set out the tomatoes on a green Fiesta-ware platter. Some were as petite as apricots and others were like hulking grapefruits, and together they formed a delightful composition.

The next day I blended the red tomatoes into a pale pink froth, then forced it through a strainer again and again, trying to be as *maadele* as possible. I took the okra out onto the porch and sat in the cool breeze, trimming the tough little stems off their caps. Most of the pods were as small as the top digit of my finger but some were like massive oversized claws. I would never have picked them in the first place except that Balkees told me her father-in-law says the big pods are the most flavorful, and that she cuts them into pieces before cooking. Yet again, I let her instructions guide me.

I tossed some finely sliced garlic in olive oil in a heavy cast iron skillet for just a few seconds, then added the okra. After it turned dark green and glistened in the oil, I smothered the okra with my tomato puree, lowered the heat and left the flavors to get acquainted. The result was as smooth as butter in tomato cream. In the end, the union of tomato and okra, *baal* and *baladi*, was made in heaven.

BAKING AND OVENS

Fassuta

It started as an idle thought. Could there be, I wondered, anyone in the Galilee today who is still growing wheat to make their own flour, olives to make their own oil, and grapes to make their own wine? If such a person existed, I imagined, chances were that I would find them in one of the more remote Christian Arab villages of the Western Galilee, up near the Lebanese border. Whenever I visit that part of the country, with its giant, ancient olive trees, crumbling citadels and emerald-sapphire Mediterranean vistas, I can almost feel the spirits of Crusaders who strayed from the nearby port of Acre almost a millennia past, to settle here and raise olives to send back to their European homes.

There was one particular village in the Western Galilee that I had in mind, a diminutive collection of homes and churches cloistered among olive-covered hills. Ever since I'd read Anton Shamas's autobiographically-inspired novel *Arabesque*, the vivid descriptions of village life in Fassuta had been etched in my imagination. Now I hoped to have a reason to visit there.

A friend of ours—a cheesemaker who lives the Western Galilee—once told me of her close relationships with villagers from

Fassuta, and I decided to give her a call. "I'm looking for some-one who is still practicing traditional agriculture in Fassuta," I explained. "Write down this number," she told me. "His name is Ayoub. He's my goat milk supplier. If anyone knows about farming in Fassuta, he does."

Ayoub listened patiently as I explained my mission. "I'm not a wine maker," he said, "but I can tell you plenty about wheat."

It was the beginning of August, a few days before my birthday, and I decided this would be the perfect opportunity to celebrate with a weekend in the Western Galilee, combining research with pleasure. Fortunately Ayoub asked us to meet him at a reasonable, mid-morning hour, after he'd finished the morning milking and Ron and I had enjoyed our bed-and-breakfast meal. The day was already blazing hot by the time we arrived at the entrance to Fas-suta where we'd agreed to meet Ayoub. He drove up in a small Jeep and we got out to greet him. Ayoub looked to be in his early sixties, lean and bronzed, with high cheekbones. In Hebrew spoken with a distinct country twang, he told us to follow him through the nar-row, twisted streets that led to his home in the heart of the village.

We parked our car next to Ayoub's and followed him up the stairs and into an extremely tidy and orderly house. Several large and handsome copper pots caught my eye, sitting on the floor among the dark wood, lace-doily-covered furniture. They had once been used in his family for cooking, Ayoub explained. He remembered as a child that a tradesman would come around to the village once a year to work some kind of treatment on everyone's copper pots so the metal wouldn't poison the food. Now, polished and empty, they served as rustic decorations. A large photo of a dramatic bride dominated one of the walls; a television tuned into a Lebanese station silently airing the news filled another. We drank the requisite coffee while I presented my credentials—a fair knowledge of edible wild plants and traditional Galilee Arab foods, and a serious desire to learn more. I knew my *ellet* and my *freekeh*, and that eased the way for the conversation that followed.

Ayoub lives with his wife and son in their family home. Their daughter—the bride on the wall—is married and lives in the center of the country with her husband and their grandchild. Ayoub once worked for the local municipality, but as his son grew older, he decided to raise goats as a project that the two of them could work on together.

Today, they have about ninety goats and a rustic but technologically modern dairy. The milk ends up being processed into camembert, feta and other varieties of goat cheese, produced in our friend's cheese-making operation. The herd also supplies the occasional goat for a special family meal, particularly on holidays. Goat, he told us, is basically the only meat they eat. It's particularly lean, he explained, and a delicacy when used to make *kubeh nieh*—pulverized raw meat combined with bulgur, or ground and seasoned to prepare kebab. "You haven't tasted anything as delicious as fresh goat," he assured us, and we admitted we had not, but hoped one day to have the opportunity.

In addition to the goats, in his spare time Ayoub and his sister Angela also grow wheat on a parcel of family land. They are, he informed me, among the last of the villagers who are still practicing this type of agriculture. I soon came to understand that it was Ayoub's sister who was his partner in carrying on the family's culinary traditions. He suggested that we go over to Angela's house, just around the corner. About ten steps across a yard that was shaded with fruit-laden grape vines and pomegranate trees, we reached her home. Angela joined us, a stout and smiling black-haired matriarch perhaps a few years younger than her brother, in a housedress, apron and slippers.

First, Ayoub showed us the cistern underneath the house where rainwater is collected during the winter, then pumped out during the long dry summer to water the *hakura*—the family vegetable garden. I described to Ayoub an image I remembered from *Arabesque* of a child being lowered into the cistern at the beginning of the summer to clean the moss off of the walls. "Sure," he said smiling. "I did that more than once." Angela grows the usual produce in her garden— tomatoes, eggplants, okra, chickpeas, fava beans and squashes—but I was amazed when Ayoub told me that she even plants lentils, the first time I'd heard of anyone in the Galilee who is still cultivating this most ancient, and labor-intensive, of local foods.

On the porch outside the entrance to the house, Ayoub hoisted up a door in the floor to reveal an underground chamber that he called the *mrateb*. "This is where we used to store tobacco after it was picked to keep it moist before packaging," he explained. Tobacco was the principal crop in Fassuta when Ayoub was growing up, and every family had a supply agreement with Israel's largest cigarette manufacturer. When the company stopped purchasing its main raw material locally, most of the villagers abandoned agriculture, and the tobacco fields were largely replanted with olive trees. There are still two or three tobacco growers left in the village, Ayoub told us, and we had in fact noticed the tobacco growing by the entrance to the village. The cigarettes Ayoub smokes are ones he rolls himself from that local tobacco—another smokavore.

Angela led us into the ground floor room of her house, a deep open space with whitewashed walls and vaulted ceiling and a spotless concrete floor, that served as a work area and storage room. A massive wooden wardrobe stood against one wall, along with other pieces of furniture that had been relegated to storage. On a table pushed up against another wall, there was a collection of different containers and tools for storing and processing foods. Hand-made wooden hoops covered with different weaves of straw mesh were piled one on top of the other, used for sifting bulgur into coarse and fine grades. Ayoub showed us a formidable block of limestone sitting on the floor with a bowl-like depression on top, and the heavy wooden mallet that went with it—the set that was used to pound raw meat when preparing *kubbeh nieh*. Even traditional Balkees, I know, prepares *kubbeh nieh* in a food processor.

A high, stainless steel box on legs with a turn-handle faucet at the bottom was used to store and dispense olive oil. Behind a curtain, rows and rows of plastic soda bottles filled with coarse and fine bulgur, chickpeas, olives and other staples were lined up on a table. Angela showed me a small plastic bottle filled with dark oil she prepares from the fruit of the bay laurel tree, which they use for scenting their home-made olive oil soap, and for rubbing into sore joints. And there was a bottle of home-made syrup, or *dibes*, made of carob, sweet for eating and effective for treating sores in the mouth.

Storing foods in recycled soda bottles is a practice I've seen all over the Galilee—not only for grains, but also for olives, pickled baby cucumbers and eggplants, and even grape leaves, stacked and folded into little balls to be pushed through the bottle opening. When the time comes to take out the contents, the top of the bottle is sawed off with a kitchen knife. I wondered how recently the transition had been made from using the pottery storage jars developed in the Neolithic era not so far from here, to the plastic soda bottle, and how many interim storage solutions were used in between. Not very long ago and not very many, I'm sure. And there, in a far corner of the room, under a pile of boxes and tools, stood one of those old clay jars. Next to it was a battered, dark metal *seah*.

That year, Ayoub told us, they still had flour left over from the previous season, so their entire wheat harvest was being used to make bulgur. The harvesting and threshing are done mechanically, but Angela still boils the clean wheat in a large pot over an open fire, then dries it in the sun for several days before the grain is cracked. For flour, they take their grain to a mill in one of the nearby villages.

"Look at this," Ayoub said, reaching into two different sacks and drawing out a small pile of wheat in each hand. The grains in one hand were elongated and dull brown, while those in the other hand were round and yellowish. "See the difference?" he asked. I saw the difference, but what it signified, I wasn't at all sure. The yellowish ones, he explained are wheat that he grew using a variety that has been in his family for generations, and that he saves to plant from season to season. The other kind was a modern variety of wheat he'd bought from a neighbor. The *freekeh*, bulgur and bread that are made from the heritage grain, he assured me, all came out better. "You can't compare the taste", he said emphatically.

I sat for a second, stunned. After my conversations with Abu Zaki, I wasn't sure if I'd ever find anyone who was still growing traditional wheat varieties. The pile of gold in his right hand suddenly took on an entirely new significance. It was not surprising that I would find this wheat here. Ayoub grows wheat for his own family's consumption, while Abu Zaki is a commercial farmer. For Abu Zaki, the higher yields of the modern hybrid varieties make up for the fact that he needs to buy new grain for planting each year. But to carry on a family tradition and produce a staple that he loves, Ayoub can afford not to compromise.

In another corner of the room sat the family *jharusheh,* the set of grindstones used to crack the grains of *freekeh* and bulgur, two ponderous disks of basalt stone from the Golan Heights, each about the diameter of a manhole cover. Here they were, still alive and grinding. To demonstrate, Ayoub and Angela hefted the top stone and threaded it onto a short pole sticking out of the middle of the bottom one. He poured a handful of grain into the hole in the middle of the top stone, and Angela took hold of a short handle set into it, and with a massive push, gave it a spin. Crushed between the two stones, the shards of grain were pushed out of shallow grooves carved into the bottom stone, and onto a cloth spread out to collect them. Depending on the desired grind, the grain would be collected and put through the stones again and again.

We left the storeroom and stepped outside into the intense sunlight, then immediately turned again into another doorway, back into darkness. As my eyes adjusted, I saw we were in a small, narrow room with high windows, where the walls and ceiling were blackened from smoke. On the cement floor on one side of the room, resting on a pile of ashes, was a *saj,* the dome-shaped metal surface used for baking the large, thin pita bread I'd always known as Druze pita. Facing it at the other side of the room, on a low stone platform, was another bread oven, but this one was a perfectly formed low igloo made of a mixture of white clay and ground straw. It was clearly hand-built by an artist; the baking chamber had an arched opening above which a small cross was shaped in bas relief. A pile of ashes remained inside the oven from the last firing. Glowing pale in the obscurity of the room, it was one of the most hauntingly beautiful pieces of handiwork I'd ever seen.

Clearly, both these ovens worked on wood. I'd seen many *sajs* and other ovens for baking pita, and almost all of them were fueled by propane gas. But Ayoub explained, he will only eat bread that is prepared on a wood fire. Otherwise it doesn't taste right.

Angela bakes bread about every two weeks and distributes it across the entire family. "We keep it in the freezer," Ayoub explained in a comfortable concession to modern ways, "and it comes out just like fresh." These days, he told us, only the adults eat the homemade bread. The kids prefer their pita bread store-bought. One day, I thought to myself, they will realize what they are missing. I asked Ayoub if I could visit one baking day. "What a question?" he said and laughed.

Baking Day

Blessed shall be your basket and your kneading bowl. Deuteronomy 28:5

Baking day in Fassuta starts early, and to get there in time, I had to leave my house just before 7:00. I was lucky to be coming during the winter; in the hot summer months, Angela and her sister-in-law, Najhla, start baking at 4:00 a.m. But on that chilly February morning, as I drove northwest, the rising sun already cast an orange glow over the olive groves, pine forests and jumble of stores in the Druze villages on either side of the road. I'd set out in an excellent mood, thanking my lucky stars that I'd embarked on this whole adventure in the first place.

Ayoub was still milking the goats when I arrived at the entrance to Fassuta, so I parked on the side of the road, watching the children with their backpacks horsing around, waiting for the school bus. Finally, Ayoub arrived and, again, I followed his Jeep through the narrow, twisting streets of the village.

This time we headed straight for Angela's house and parked next to the entrance to the baking room. Through the open door, behind a haze of smoke, I could discern Angela and Najhla, an older woman with grey hair held back in a kerchief, working the dough on the *saj*. The women greeted me with smiles of recognition. Today they were preparing the immense, paper-thin pita bread that I knew of as Druze pita, which they called *elrif*.

Taking a deep breath, I stepped inside the smoky room and sat down on a low stool, out of their way, to watch. The women sat on the floor facing one another, their legs spread and their bare feet almost touching. The space between them was filled with a low wooden work surface powdered with flour. Angela had her back to the wall, and the concave metal *saj* with a lively fire burning underneath it was separated from her left leg by a single row of bricks. A cloth-covered tray holding balls of dough was tucked up to her right leg, next to a growing stack of finished *elrif*.

Early that morning, they had prepared and rolled out dough for about 200 *elrif*, enough to keep the family in bread for the next few weeks. These days they use commercially-produced yeast, but they remember when bread was made with a starter, a fist-sized lump taken from the previous batch of dough, wrapped in a cloth and stored in the flour bin.

Angela reached underneath the cloth that covered the tray to take out a powdery pale dough ball, covered by a thin coat of bran saved from the flour milling, to keep the balls from sticking together. She gave the ball a preliminary flattening on the board in front of her, then handed it to Najhla. After twirling it in the air like a pizza chef, she placed the thin disk in the center of a broad, floppy round pillow about the circumference of a car tire. She deftly tugged on the edges of the dough until it covered the entire surface of the pillow, and then handed the pillow back to Angela. With a swift flip, Angela tossed the dough from the pillow onto the scorching surface of the *saj*. Instantly large bubbles appeared across its surface, making it look like an inverted moonscape, and the pale dough turned golden in front of my eyes. During the minute or two of baking, Angela started in on the next ball and Najhla tended the fire, adding another branch of oak from a pile in the corner when needed. When the *elrif* was done, with her bare hands, Angela swept it off the *saj* and onto the pile at her side.

I watched the metamorphosis of dough as it was passed from hand to hand and to the fire, in an easy, genial rhythm. "Baking in the winter requires double the amount of yeast," Angela explained. "But the bread comes out better. And as the old saying goes," she said, laughing, "people who bake bread in the winter don't need to be paid; enjoying the heat of the stove is compensation enough." It was indeed warm and cozy in the little room, although tears were streaming from my eyes from the smoke.

I asked about the second oven behind me, the exquisite one made of white clay. Who built it? I wanted to know. Angela pointed to her sister-in-law, who looked away shyly. "She made it a few years ago."

"And where did the earth to build it come from?" I asked.

"There's a place in the village that is a good source for clay," Angela explained. "She knows where it is." I wondered if Najhla's knowledge of how to build ovens out of earth, most probably learned from her mother, had been passed on. The clay oven, which they called a *furen*, is used to bake the more familiar, standard-sized pita bread. Perhaps the next time they baked, she told me, they would work on that one. I hoped that one day I'd be able to join them, and see it lit up from the inside.

Ayoub had gone off and now returned with his son and a tray on which all the ingredients for breakfast were balanced. There was a plate with ivory spheres of labaneh resting like moist cocoons in a pool of green olive oil, another dish of *zaatar* mixture, and a third, with cracked olives speckled with flecks of red pepper. There was also a stick of margarine and a bowl of sugar for the baking-day treat that Ayoub and his son were waiting for. Angela prepared two special pitas for her brother and nephew, thicker and smaller than the others, and baked them on the *saj* until they were golden brown. As Angela handed him each finished pita, Ayoub rubbed it with the margarine and sprinkled it with sugar, folded it in half and handed the first one to his son, then did the same for himself.

I had decided to forego the sweet, and savored my fresh *elrif* with the *labaneh*, *zaatar* and olives. Ayoub showed me how to fold pieces torn off from the expanse of pita into a manageable package, then scoop up the *labaneh* and dip it into the *zaatar*. The pure pleasure from each of the flavors was intensified by the appreciation that everything I was eating was a product of this family's labors. I asked Ayoub if he ever went a day without eating bread. "Unimaginable," he replied.

Baking on Stones

*He looked about; and there, beside his head, was a cake baked
on hot stones and a jar of water!* 1 Kings 19:6

Cooking dough on stones heated in a fire is the most ancient form of
baking known to humankind. At Ohalo II, the site of a Paleolithic-
era settlement of hunters and gatherers on the shores of the Sea of
Galilee, a number of circular stone hearths were discovered under a
thick layer of silt. One of those hearths stood out among the others,
its interior entirely lined with stones. Could this, the archaeologists
speculated, be the earliest oven on record?

Another larger stone from the site, tentatively identified as a
grindstone, was sent to the Smithsonian Institute for testing. Using
starch particle analysis, microscopic crumbs extracted from inden-
tations in the stone were identified as wild barley and wheat. This
finding represented the earliest unequivocal evidence of grain being processed—ostensibly to be mixed with water, patted into cakes
and set onto one of the heated stones in the nearby hearth.

Twenty-four thousand years later, in a farming village a few
short miles away from the Ohalo II site, the bread baking on stones
continues. Tova, the mother of a friend, rolls out handfuls of soft

white dough and flattens them into discs next to a pre-heated outdoor oven in her backyard. Inside the oven, which her husband Amit built out of bricks smoothed over with concrete according to her specifications, several pieces of kindling are burning. Next to them, in the oven's dark interior, a small cluster of stones, huddled together like eggs in a nest, are soaking up the heat.

Tova gathered these stones herself from the shores of the Sea of Galilee, she explains. Each one is the size of a duck's egg, smooth and spherical. When Tova's mother immigrated to Israel from Morocco in the 1950s, she gave up her practice of baking in an outdoor oven. But on the floor of her new gas oven, she still kept a circle of stones on which she baked the traditional Moroccan bread known as *frena*. Tova's mother was a legendary cook, and worked in the kitchens of several hotels in Safed. It was her mother who taught Tova that when you bake bread, you have to love the dough when you work with it.

Tova and Amit, now in their early 50s, have been farming in the Galilee since the 1970s. They started raising poultry; then, when the bottom fell out of that market, they moved on to cultivating mangoes. When the market winds shifted yet again, they replanted the sloping hillside around their home with grapevines. One of the major Israeli wineries purchases the fruit of their vineyard every year. But they always leave just enough for Amit to distill his own wine and the local anise-flavored brandy called Arak.

Tova uses a long-handled wooden paddle to slide a circle of dough over the hot stones, where it instantly collapses, taking on their lumpy contours. Within two minutes the first side is done and Tova reaches in with a gloved hand to deftly flip the loaf so it can brown on the other side. One more minute and the bread is out, golden and steaming hot, with five egg-like protrusions. We tear off crusty white clouds, then dip them in an aromatic green relish that Tova has made from the *zaatar* that she grows in her garden, cooked in olive oil pressed from the fruit of their own trees. The flavors of earth and sky merge in each mouthful.

The *Tabun*

For a long time we wanted to build our own wood-burning oven out in the back yard. The generic name that's used these days for such ovens is *tabun*. But as Um Malek once explained to me, the *tabun* she remembers was an entire outbuilding inside which an earthen oven burned round the clock, and which served the cooking needs of an entire neighborhood. When homes had no electricity, which in some Arab villages in the Galilee was well into the 1980s, cooking and baking was done over fire, and ovens large and small were built out of local clay mixed with ground-up straw.

A woman I know who has traveled across Israel and India learning how to build ovens once told me that the gesture of mixing earth and water to create an oven is like mixing flour and water to produce bread dough. The simplest materials are transformed in this small act of alchemy.

Balkees remembers her mother building a *khebazi*, a smaller oven especially for baking bread. Mother and children would set out on excursions to collect clay from a special source on a hillside. Using a large, cut-open tin can as a mold, she would build up the walls of the oven with clay every day, layer by layer, until the sides came together at the top. The *khebazi* would last several years, until another had to be made. It's been decades since anyone in Balkees's family has cooked on a *khebazi*.

There were several forces driving our *tabun*-building project. Mainly, I wanted to add our small contribution to perpetuating the age-old practice of building clay ovens. But I also wanted to involve my friends in the project. It would be another topic to discuss with Um Malek. A project to work on with Balkees. And since there seemed to be a sweeping consensus that nothing is as delicious as food cooked over a wood fire, I knew that, with the *tabun*, entertaining guests at home would be foolproof.

The model for our *tabun* was the one our friend Mahmoud had built at his country-house outside of Turan. One Saturday morning, we set out to his village on a fact-finding mission, the first step towards bringing our *tabun* from the conceptual to the three-dimensional. As we neared the house, a thin spiral of smoke signaled that the *tabun* was already on duty.

Several years ago Mahmoud transformed a piece of agricultural land he inherited outside his village into a *bustan*, a private Garden of Eden with a vegetable plot, fruit trees, a fountain and a little house to relax in. For Mahmoud, it was a place to work in the garden and entertain family and friends, with nothing but green to fill one's eyes. The house is surrounded by a covered porch, overgrown with passion fruit vines, and in one corner, stands the *tabun*.

Built on top of a waist-high platform, the *tabun* looks like a barrel sliced vertically and laid on its side, covered in smooth, yellow clay. At the front, a metal door opens onto a smoky-black interior, with a metal shelf in the middle. A small wood fire burned underneath it, on the concrete base. We studied the *tabun* from every angle and took detailed measurements. Afterwards, we sat on the porch drinking icy pomegranate juice, discussing the overall plan. Mahmoud, ever ready to embark on a new project, offered to oversee its construction.

The first step was to decide where to put the *tabun*. It couldn't be too close to the neighbor's house, who might be bothered by the smoke. There had to be enough room on which to build an ample base for the *tabun* and a workspace next to it. And it had to be close to the house but not too close. Ron paced the yard with a tape measure, setting stakes into the ground to test out different spots.

Once the site was chosen, two builders, Druze men from Daliat el Carmel, were given the sketched-out plans, and in three days, they built the base out of cement blocks and covered it with plaster. The top of the platform and the work surface were about waist high, and an open space was left underneath, which would eventually be fitted with shelves and a door.

In the meantime, Ron and Mahmoud spent hours with our friend Tzvika, a carpenter with the know-how and tools for welding, building a metal frame for the *tabun*. Thin pieces of particle board were bent and affixed along the frame's concave interior walls. They would support the clay until it dried, and burn away with the first firing. The outside of the frame would be covered with chicken wire. On the front of the frame, they welded a metal door on hinges.

While the builders spread fresh concrete onto the top platform, Ron and Mahmoud set the metal frame into the wet material, positioning it with a level. A friend and I placed pieces of broken pottery into the concrete of the work surface next to the oven to create a mosaic. Another milestone reached.

The actual work of covering the *tabun* with clay would be done by Abu Jouni, a friend of Mahmoud's from Nazareth. He was the one who built Mahmoud's *tabun* and had agreed to do ours as well. But before he could start, we needed to supply the building material—clay and straw.

The workshop of Nazareth's only remaining pottery manufacturer is not far from Balkees's home. These days, they produce small clay oil lamps and other souvenirs that are sold in the tourist shops, but at one time they specialized in the clay cooking pots that were standard kitchen workhorses before the advent of aluminum and stainless steel pots. Much of the clay they work with is dug out of the hill behind their shop. Balkees's husband Muhammad persuaded his neighbor to support the *tabun* effort, and he agreed to let their oldest son Jouad dig out ten small sacks of clay for us, which Muhammad delivered to our house.

The clay was crumbly dry and deep ochre. The builders had left a large plastic barrel with the top cut off, into which Mahmoud emptied several of the bags of clay. He then poured water over it all, leaving an extra several inches on top. The clay would need to soften over two days, after which it would be ready to work with. Ron brought a large sack of straw from the dairy.

On a bright Friday morning, Mahmoud arrived with his teenage son Kareem, followed in a separate car by Abu Jouni and his brother Abu Samer. Dressed in freshly-pressed work clothes, they immediately set to work emptying tools and equipment from the trunk of their car.

The two men looked to be in their late sixties, and were a study in contrasts. Abu Jouni was the younger and taller of the two brothers, with thinning hair at the sides of his bald head, and a broad, white-toothed smile. His older brother was slight and serious, with a thick head of wiry grey hair. They spoke in Arabic with Mahmoud, discussing the plan for the day. Ron had to be at work that morning, so I was left in charge of supplying whatever would be needed.

Before they could get started, Mahmoud explained, they had to "grease the machinery." From the back seat of his car Abu Samer took out a bag with a dozen fresh rolls, a package of sliced yellow cheese, a can of pickles, and a bottle of Arak. I set out sliced tomatoes and a bowl of olives, and we shared a convivial breakfast on the porch of our house, washed down with glasses of milky Arak diluted in water.

As Abu Jouni watched, Kareem dredged the satiny gold wet clay up out of the barrel with a pail and poured it like thick paint into a trough that the brothers had brought. Then he switched to a shovel to mix it with sand and straw until it reached the consistency that Abu Jouni was satisfied with. They loaded the clay mixture into buckets and the two brothers spread it with trowels over the chicken wire base like thick frosting. Working on either side, they applied layer after layer. Once it had taken days to build an oven, Abu Jouni told me. Now, with the frame and its supports, they would be able to finish the work in a single morning.

Until he retired, Abu Jouni had been a handyman at the Catholic Church and school in Tsippori, just outside of Nazareth. His brother was a retired electrician. They told me that they had learned how to build with clay in their youth, from watching their parents.

These days, building in clay is only a hobby, something they do for family and friends.

While Abu Jouni rested in the shade, I took his place, smoothing the cool clay and straw with my bare hands along the curved surface. Life has to be enjoyed, Abu Jouni announced, and Abu Samer nodded in agreement. He and his four brothers are always hosting family meals or going out hunting for wild boar. Health issues can be overcome, and financial worries put aside, he said. But life is short and to be relished. Everyone who had a glass in hand raised it.

The *tabun*, now dressed in its thick yellow coat, was left to dry in the sun for several days before the first firing. The firing process needed to be gradual, and Mahmoud came to supervise. He and Ron huddled around the open metal door, tending the flame, and watching the clay crack as it expanded. Over the weeks to come, layer upon layer was added, and still the cracks appeared with every burning.

But cracks seemed inevitable and eventually the *tabun* needed to be inaugurated. Since no one who had been involved in the creation of the *tabun* was willing to accept payment, we decided to host them all for a festive *tabun* meal—the kind of party feast summed up in Arabic as a *hafla*.

• • •

After consulting with Balkees, we called the *hafla* for Friday lunch, a time that took into account the weekend routines of everyone involved. We decided that the most festive fare for the occasion would be lamb. Balkees suggested stuffed lamb collar, a dish I'd seen on the menu of finer Arab restaurants, and which she assured us was one of her specialties. She would show us how to prepare the lamb, and oversee the cooking in the *tabun*.

On Thursday evening, Muhammad took Ron to his friend the butcher in Nazareth to buy the lamb, according to Balkees's specifications. Ron returned home that night wielding a heavy plastic bag, with two elongated cuts of meat. The next morning it was my turn to drive to Nazareth, to pick up Balkees and bring her back to the house. When I showed up at her door, she was already waiting, with a pot of grape leaves stuffed with *freekeh* that she'd rolled the night before, and several shopping bags filled with various containers and utensils.

In my kitchen, we each tied aprons around our waists and started on the filling for the lamb. I toasted slivered almonds in olive oil, then added pine nuts, which, as Balkees explained to me, have a shorter toasting time. In a separate pot, she browned finely ground beef, leaving it to cook until all the liquid disappeared. We measured, washed, and drained rice, then added it to a large mixing bowl with the ground beef and nuts, black pepper and the *baharat* spice mixture of black pepper, allspice, cinnamon and the other secret ingredients that Balkees favors.

The butcher had removed the bones from the lamb, trimmed away much of the extra fat, and sliced a pocket for the stuffing. Balkees rubbed the meat inside and out with salt, pepper and *baharat*, then filled the cavity with the rice mixture. Then she pulled the edges of the opening together and closed it with toothpicks around which she wove a piece of thread. We set the roll of meat inside a pot with a quartered onion for company, then covered it all with water.

In the meantime, Ron had a lively fire going in the *tabun*. Balkees arranged four eggplants among the embers, after giving each one a single stab. She only agreed to take them out when they were black and flaky; trying not to burn our fingers, we peeled away the charred skin to scrape out the soft white flesh inside.

Cooking in my kitchen, working with such choice ingredients and on this festive occasion, put Balkees in an excellent mood. The mentor in her came shining through as she explained each step and the rationale behind it. Between following her instructions, I scribbled notes, thinking that I was enjoying this part of the festivities at least as much as I would the actual meal.

Once the eggplants were dispensed with, two oval roasting pans went into the *tabun*, the first with the lamb and the second filled with chicken pieces tucked into a bed of chopped onion, carrots, and zucchini. The chicken would take about an hour, the lamb, double that time. The grape leaves were cooking on the stove, weighted down with a plate and a bowl filled with water on top of it.

The only thing left to prepare was the salads. We sorted, cleaned and chopped bunches of peppery *jarjir* and green onion. In a separate bowl we mixed coarsely chopped tomato, cucumber, parsley and lettuce. I seasoned the salads with olive oil, lemon juice, sumac and salt, then started to toss them with my salad spoons. "Some things you have to feel with your hands, even before you taste them," Balkees remarked pointedly. I put the spoons aside and plunged my hands down to the bottom of the bowl, then lightly tossed the greens until they were slick with the sumac-grainy oil. Only then did I taste a crunchy sour mouthful. It would be the perfect foil for the rich, spiced lamb.

Everyone who had contributed to making the *tabun* was invited to the *hafla*. First to arrive were Abu Jouni and Abu Samer, followed by Mahmoud, his wife and son. Tzvika came with his wife, and finally Muhammad and their youngest son. Even though I'd told everyone not to bring anything, bottles of wine were extended, as well as a tray of baklava and a plastic soda bottle full of homemade pickles.

We ate our meal on the back porch, in plain view of the smoking *tabun*, which had developed several new cracks. Not to worry, Abu Jouni said. "Just let it work. We'll fix it another day."

The lamb came out of the *tabun* brown and crispy. Thick slices of tender, marbled meat and rice disappeared from the serving platter, and the men washed them down with beer and Arak. The roasted eggplant, which Balkees had mixed with crushed fresh spring garlic, was passed around. Abu Samer helped himself to more stuffed grape leaves, clearly delighted at the unexpected culinary virtuosity of this feast.

The conversation flowed, shifting back and forth between Hebrew and Arabic. Ron stood up and made a toast, thanking everyone who had helped bring our *tabun* into the world. To top off the meal, Balkees prepared *knaffeh*. She had melted butter in a large baking tray onto which she laid down a generous layer of the thin filaments of dough called *kaddaif*, pressing on it until she felt the butter soaking through to her fingers. On top of that, she sprinkled a layer of *jibni*—mild white goat cheese made by Um S—that I'd grated, and on top of that, another layer of *kaddaif*.

She and Ron fit the baking sheet into the *tabun* and within minutes it was done. They inverted the *knaffeh* onto a platter, brown and crispy, and poured lemon-geranium-scented syrup on top. People are passionate about *knaffeh* because it offers such a complex balance of flavors and textures—the crunchy bottom layer of *kaddaif* against the smoother inner layer. The sweetness of the syrup and the saltiness of the *jibni*. The perfume of the lemon-geranium and the richness of the butter. All conversation fell silent in deference to this grand dessert.

Balkees had made *knaffeh* many times before, she told me. But this was her first time making it in a *tabun*. She was more than satisfied with the results.

Now she has her own idea hatching, to build a *tabun* in her brother's yard in Kfar Reine. "Your mother can help you," I suggested. "Don't you think she still remembers how to do it?"

"Of course she does," Balkees replied.

GRAPES AND
SUMMER YIELDS

Fig Cakes

Abigail quickly got together two hundred loaves of bread, two jars of wine, five dressed sheep, five seahs of parched [grain], one hundred cakes of raisin, and two hundred cakes of pressed figs. 1 Samuel 25:18

It took no small amount of convincing to get M to agree to meet me. I'd read about him and his expertise in drying figs, and I was interested in hearing about a practice that seemed to me to trace directly back to the Bible and the fig cakes that Abigail supplied to David and his band in exile. Since that article about him had appeared in the paper, M told me irately on the phone, all manner of people had started to bother him, and he didn't want any more publicity. I assured him that I would not publish his name, and that I only wanted to learn more about his way with figs. With a sigh, he finally agreed, and gave me directions to his house in the village of Jish, or as it is known in ancient and contemporary Hebrew, Gush Halav.

The historic quarter of Jish is a jumble of stone homes, twisting streets, an ancient synagogue and doll-house-scale churches perched at the top of a hill. At its summit, the sheer density of ancient ruins in the layers of earth has led the Antiquities Authority to declare the area off limits for building. So, instead of houses on one of the highest spots of the village, there is a small, haphazard orchard of cherries, apples, peaches and the figs for which Jish is renowned in these parts.

The natural springs near Jish have attracted human settlement at least since the Bronze Age, and standing next to a fig tree, with so many layers of history under one's sandals, it's hard not to feel as ephemeral as this season's fruit. Crossing the orchard, in the crumble of stones underfoot, I glimpsed a small carved fragment—two perfect scrolls broken off of a Corinthian capital.

We found M's house near the entrance to the village, and he greeted us at the door, a pleasant-looking man in his 40s, with light green eyes and a balding head. We stepped out of the bright heat of the summer day into the cool, dark interior of a spacious, newly-built home. M led us to the family room where his four daughters were lounging on couches in front of a large TV, the smallest two napping. His wife, H, joined us, and I explained to them who I was and what had brought me to Jish. As I spoke, I could see the suspicion slowly fading from M's face. Then he began to talk.

He had grown up in this village, and although his family had little means, his memories were of a rich and happy time. They were, and still are, a Muslim family in a predominantly Christian village, and the relations between the neighbors were, and still are, amicable. In his childhood, there was no electricity, and the food they ate was what they grew and what they stored.

M remembered every season and its labors. In the summer, he would help his mother collect the figs that grow so abundantly around the village. They would dry them in the sun, covered with branches of dried wild fennel to protect the sugar-laden fruit. Once the figs were dry enough, they would string them like beads onto long hoops and hang them in the basement. Some of the dried figs would be pressed into brick-like blocks, recruiting M's portly uncle to sit on the wooden press for good measure. These, I surmised, were the fig cakes of the Bible.

He also learned from his mother how to prepare the thick brown fig syrup called *dibes*. M remembered two containers built into the wall in the family's kitchen—one with olive oil and the other with *dibes*. "When I wanted something sweet, I was given bread with *dibes*. That's the only candy I knew."

Now, with village life so radically changed, M is determined to preserve some remnants of his childhood life. On early summer mornings, he rouses his children and takes them down to the *wadi* where the native *biyaddi* fig trees are full of fruit. That's the best time to pick, when the air is still cool and the morning dew dissolves the sticky milk that oozes from the freshly picked fruit and can make your skin itch. Back at the house, each fig is gently squeezed from the bottom so that it spreads open like a flower. After that, they are laid out on a sheet on the flat rooftop to dry in the sun for three days.

M led us up to the roof of the house, where figs were spread out in layers on a tarp. In another corner of the rooftop, small red sumac berries were also drying in the sun. They, too, are in season during high summer, and M and his family had collected them from bushes that grow wild in these parts. Once the berries are dry, M rubs them across a metal sieve, producing the wine-colored sumac powder that is a highly valued, potently sour spice.

Coming down from the roof, we sat on the back porch of the house, where much of the fig processing work is done. A plate of fresh figs was on the table. The name for this particular variety, *bi-yaddi*, is derived from the Arabic word for the color white and refers to the light hue of the fruit—green as opposed to the purple or "black" varieties. They are small, rotund, and light green, with a deep crimson inner flesh. This particular variety thrives on very little water—only what comes from the heavens—hence the intensity of their flavor. Their low moisture content also makes them ideal for drying. H brought a basket of fresh pita bread and dishes of *dibes* for us to dip into. The flavor was similar to molasses, only lighter and more fruity.

To make fig cakes, M uses his own fig press which he had custom-made—a small, open stainless-steel box fitted with a screw lever. He filled a plastic bag with dried figs, fit it into the press, then twisted the screw to compress the fruit. Out came a marbled ingot of dried figs that, if sliced judiciously, would last until the following summer.

M and H also make *dibes* according to his mother's system. They start by soaking the dried figs in water for twelve hours, and then discard the fruit (although he remembered it once being used for animal feed). The next morning, they put up the liquid to simmer in a large pot over an open fire. Towards evening, when a tantalizing smell fills the air and the syrup glides off a spoon in a slow, steady stream, the *dibes* is ready.

These days, the family's clear fig favorite is *mahoud*, a jam H prepares from dried figs, fortified with sesame seeds and walnuts, all locally grown. At the time I was there, in early August, it was still too early in the season to prepare *mahoud*, which gave me a good reason to plan a return visit.

Back home, I sliced a thin layer of fig cake to taste. The flavor of the dried fruit was delicately sweet, chewy and remarkably close to fresh—with none of the mustiness I'd come to expect from dried figs. In fact, the only feature in common between the two versions that I could find was the pleasant crunch of seeds between my teeth.

Under the Grape Vine

...everyone under his own vine and under his own fig tree. 1 Kings 5:5

In the historic heart of the Druze village of Beit Jann, the centuries-old, low stone houses are connected to each other wall-to-wall, neighbor-to-neighbor. This saved on building materials that were laborious to procure, provided security against unwanted intruders, and reinforced a closely-knit social fabric. But what this approach to building didn't always take into account was the need of every home to have its own grape arbor.

Why was having your own grape vine so important, even when there was no wine being made? For pleasant shade, certainly, and for sultry summer nights spent under starlight filtering through the leaves. And for the sweet seasonal pleasure of the fruit of the vine, eaten as is, dried to make raisins, or cooked into *dibes*, syrup to be savored when the vine was bare. But perhaps most importantly, a healthy, lush grapevine ensured a daily supply of fresh, tender grape leaves, only steps away from the kitchen, to prepare *dawali*. For no summer meal is complete without a dish of lemony, rice-and-ground-meat-filled grape leaves.

When ingenuity meets nature, almost any problem can be

overcome. The resourceful families of Beit Jann simply trained their grape vines up the exterior walls of the houses, all the way up to an arbor built on the flat roof. Walking the narrow, twisting streets of old Beit Jann, you can see these vines, thick as tree trunks, emerging out of small patches of earth left uncovered by concrete, and snaking up the walls of the houses. Reaching the roof, they continue skyward, then veer sharply from their course to spread out like lace across a horizontal trellis. Only at that rooftop terminus is the sturdy vine's energy diverted to produce branches, leaves and fruit.

Set high on a densely-forested peak of the Meron Mountain range, Beit Jann is one of a dozen Druze villages in the Upper Galilee. For centuries the Druze were a persecuted minority in the Muslim-dominated landscape, and they built their villages on strategically defensible mountaintops. Their agricultural land extended beyond the perimeters of the city walls, down the mountain slopes and into the valleys below.

Over time, the village expanded in concentric circles out of its historic heart as, one by one, parcels of agricultural land belonging to Beit Jann's thirty-two clans were cleared of their crop rows to build homes for young families. Even today, amidst the patchwork sprawl of new homes, scattered open lots are still planted with summer vegetables, olive trees and grape vines, at least for the time being.

The mountain air in Beit Jann is brisk and invigorating and it seems to permeate the village with a buzzing energy. Women in dark, calf-length dresses and tights, their hair covered in white scarves, slip in and out of storefronts and doorways, while men on tractors and SUVs negotiate the hairpin turns of the narrow, hilly streets. Druze men who are committed to a religiously observant life cover their heads—either with a white knit cap or a colorfully-embroidered one—and wear traditional, baggy-legged pantaloons, gathered neatly at the ankle. Their religious ritual is wrapped in mystery, privy only to its practitioners.

My friend Salman Dabbour is not a religious man, but he was born in Beit Jann, has lived here for most of his fifty-something years, and is steeped in Druze culture. Like many Druze men, he served in the Israeli military, retiring as a high-ranking officer. He was also one of the first from Beit Jann to get a university degree. Today, Salman runs a community center serving the neighboring Druze villages of Yanuch and Jat.

Salman's parents moved out of the crowded core of the village in the 1950s and built the house he grew up in, overlooking the forest and the *wadi*, near one of the three springs which once supplied water to those without access to their own well. Even when Salman and his new wife chose a piece of land just a few yards from his parents on which to build their own home, it was still at the periphery of the village. Since then, the village limits have reached and overtaken them, but from Salman's living room window, he can still see where the houses give way to narrow stretches of tilled fields extending between the mountain slopes, where grape trellises and olive trees thrive in the cool altitude. A stream wends its way through the *wadi*, and thorny blackberry bushes line its banks.

The entrance to Salman's rambling, gracious home passes under a pair of grape arbors positioned at the front door and the back porch. On the late summer day I visited him, fat clusters of purple and green grapes hung over our heads like extravagant chandeliers. In Arabic, grapes, like figs, are described in monochromatic terms—they are either black, designating purple fruit, or white, for green. Beit Jann, Salman told me, was once famous for its grapes, particularly the white *imdawar*, a variety with perfectly round fruit that inspired its name, and the *tfakhi*, black and as large as small apples, which would stay fresh on the vine until January.

During the season, Salman's parents used to load their donkey with fruit to sell in Safed. But a *phylloxera* scourge in the 1960s decimated these local varieties, leaving the local farmers to try their luck with the Dabuki and Moneymaker grape varieties promoted by the Agriculture Ministry. By then, however, the younger generations of Beit Jann men were opting for more lucrative career opportunities in the armed forces, and agriculture became a peripheral pastime.

Salman's father tended his *hakura* on a piece of family land until the day he died, and Salman continues to cultivate it, stubbornly thwarting any family member with building ambitions. As he weeds, hoes and harvests, Salman carries on conversations with his father and cultivates the roots his parents and grandparents invested in this soil. When we spoke, Salman's *hakura* was producing cabbages and cauliflower, zucchini and tomatoes, black-eyed peas and, of course, grapes. He distributes the yields across the extended family, and rarely do they need to buy vegetables from a store.

Drawing from its Zoroastrian origins, the Druze religion embraces the concept of reincarnation, and Salman is waiting patiently for his father's soul to reappear and cross his path. Once a Druze, always a Druze, in what could be one of the most exclusive societies on earth. The body, Salman explained to me, is like a shirt, which is tossed away when it isn't needed anymore. The spirit, however, is already trying a new one on for size.

Salman's father could barely read and write, and his mother, not at all. He studied for his matriculation exams under the light of a kerosene lamp, and all of his six children are either university graduates or destined for higher education. The Dabbour family flourishes, generation after generation, in the Druze microcosm of Beit Jann, even as the world around them is transformed. "In the past," Salman explained to me, "we lived under a constant existential threat from hostile outsiders. Today, education is the key to our survival."

Salman is imbued with the comfortable ease that comes from having his spiritual and geographic coordinates perfectly aligned. But though she keeps herself as invisible as she can, Salman Dabbour's wife is the backbone of his empire, and he adamantly reminds me of her centrality to their lives. Shying away from company in the recesses of their house, surrounded by daughters and grandchildren, she is the caretaker of the private traditions of a Druze family home. When every family meal is eaten at home, out of ingredients that make their way from the surrounding landscape into her kitchen virtually without intermediary, she is never still.

Salman's wife makes rounds of fresh white farmer's cheese to be sliced and drizzled with olive oil, pressed from the fruit of the family's olive trees. She supervises the process of boiling, drying and milling wheat to make bulgur. Out of that bulgur, she makes delightful little pancakes, adorned with fried onion and sprinkled with sumac, that I've seen only on her table. And if she doesn't pick the grape leaves for *dawali* herself, then you know she has sent Salman to do it for her. Because that is how things are done here, even now.

A Vineyard Planted

All the best of the new oil, wine and grain—the choice parts that
they present to the Lord—I give to you. Numbers 18:12

Scholars of food history have given a name to the holy triumvirate of
wheat, olives and grapes, calling it "the Mediterranean triad." The domestication of these three indigenous foods in this part of the world,
they claim, was responsible for nothing less than the emergence of
Western civilization. And if wheat fueled the process, and oil greased
the wheels, it was wine that offered up the vision and hope—and
revealed the folly—of building an orderly human society.

The shallow treading press carved into a conveniently slanting
slab of limestone at the entrance to the Alonei Aba Nature Reserve
suggests that, several millennia ago, grapes were most likely grown
in this area to produce wine. Equally plausibly, it was the Jewish
and Christian residents who frequented their respective houses of
worship, excavated up the hill in Beit Lehem Haglilit, who made
their own sacramental wine here during the first centuries of the
Common Era.

When they built the agricultural foundations of Waldheim
in the early 1900s, the Templers planted a vineyard and produced

wine, leaving behind them a dusty collection of basket-covered glass demijohns in the cellar of the village creamery. The Romanian newcomers continued to cultivate the vineyard, and our neighbor Puyo, a slight, sharp-beaked old man true to his nickname "little chicken," was responsible for turning its grapes into an income generator for the village.

After he retired, Puyo began to produce his own wine. Every summer harvest, he had several cartons of grapes delivered from the vineyard to his yard. Rolling up his trouser legs, he'd tread those grapes in a plastic tub, skinny-ankle deep in skins and juice. He poured the liquid into one of the German glass jars, rigged with a tangle of plastic tubes to release the gases of fermentation. And every year, full of neighborly good will, Puyo would offer us a bottle of his home-made vintage. We found Puyo's wine undrinkable, but he savored it all year long with the satisfaction that came from his intimate acquaintance with each variety of grape he had nurtured, and the ground out of which it emerged.

Alonei Aba continues to grow grapes today—Cabernet, Muscat and Shiraz, destined for the vast vats of Carmel Mizrachi, the godfather of modern Israel's wine industry. But one section of the vineyard is reserved for White Muscat and Dabuki table grapes which are distributed to the moshav members every Friday throughout the summer season.

•   •   •

Noah, the tiller of the soil, was the first to plant a vineyard. Genesis 9:20

These days, when producing quality wine is a high-stakes mixture of art and science, the simple formula of growing grapes, squeezing out their juice, and leaving it to ferment no longer suffices. In matters of *terroir*, one must travel significantly further north of the Jezreel Valley, to the brisk altitudes of the Upper Galilee, to find the grape-growing conditions artisanal winemakers so avidly seek.

Gaby Sadan, a ruddy, soft-spoken farmer with a head of copper curls, was one of the first to explore the wine-producing potential of the Upper Galilee and Golan Heights in the late 1990s. After a decade of viticulture immersion in France, Sonoma, and South Australia, Gaby came back to Israel with a fine-tuned sensibility for the nuances of growing grapes with the characteristics that make premium wines. He built a distinguished career as a wine maker for several top wineries, at a time when Israeli wines were establishing their place in the international fine wine community. Then he put it all aside to return to his original passion. Gaby Sadan decided to plant his own vineyard.

> *My beloved had a vineyard*
> *On a fruitful hill*
> *He broke the ground, cleared it of stones*
> *and planted it with choice vines...* Isaiah 5:1-2

In a process laden with fateful decisions, large and small, Gaby's first task was to find a choice piece of land on which to set down stakes. After walking dozens of potential sites, he settled on one just as much for its beauty as for the qualities of its soil. Extending over some twenty-five acres of rolling hills bounded by thick oak forests, straddling the border between the Western and Upper Galilees, this isolated patch of land treats anyone working on it to expansive, face-to-face views of majestic Mount Hermon and the distant hills of Lebanon. While the hills obscure any glimpse of the Mediterranean,

193

the sea's proximity is palpable in the cool afternoon breezes that blow in from the west.

Thanks to its hilly topography, Gaby's vineyard has its own microclimate, with rainfall significantly higher than areas only a few acres away. And while much of the grape growing in the Upper Galilee is done in *terra rossa* and lime-permeated soils, in this particular spot, the earth is thick with flint. This, Gaby knew, would guarantee good drainage during the winter rains. With each of the three cardinal parameters of growing grapes for wine—soil, exposure, and climate—he was satisfied.

Before he could plant, though, the land had to be made ready. Working by hand with a small team, they cleared it of the larger stones, leaving a judicious layer of native flint. Then they laid the irrigation lines and stakes upon which the vines would be trained to climb.

Gaby discovered from meteorological data that his piece of land was climatically in sync with Southern France. Already passionate about French winemaking, he decided to make the most of this auspicious geographical affinity, and planted the land with Grenache, Mourvedre and Syrah.

Growing grapes for wine involves a delicate orchestration of energy between the vine and the fruit. Adding fertilizer, for example, will produce a heartier vine and plentiful fruit. Making do without it, however, as Gaby does, leaves the vine to draw its nutrients solely from those found in its particular bit of earth. It will have to struggle harder, and will yield less fruit. But the grapes it does produce will eloquently express in their flavor every natural element that nurtured them. Handled attentively, these qualities will shine through in the wine. The connection between the soil, the sky, the vine, the fruit and the wine press is integral and inseparable. That is why Gaby considers himself a wine grower.

. . .

Gaby says that this is a crazy year. But then, he adds, every year is a crazy year. The fact remains, however, that last year he harvested his Barbera grapes on the 8th of August, and here we were in mid-September and only now were the same grapes ready to be picked. My last visit to the vineyard had been in winter, when Mount Hermon in the distance was covered in snow and the fledgling shoots of vine were bare sticks, calf-high. Now the densely verdant vines towered over my head. Nestled among their leaves, as lush and perfect as Tiffany glass, the fat purple clusters hung quiet and compliant, awaiting their destiny. All of the work of the entire year, Gaby explained, was focused on this moment.

Harvesting had started early, in the lingering nighttime chill. By 10 a.m., the relentless late-summer sun would begin to heat up the grapes, so the work had to be done quickly. A fortified team of about a dozen Druze workers was doing the picking, older men with long bushy grey mustaches, women in long skirts with leggings underneath, and young men, pierced and tattooed, all joking and laughing among the rows. They eyed me with mild curiosity, and Gaby explained that I am a writer. The general consensus seemed to be that I was harmless enough.

Gaby's decision to forego machines and harvest by hand is yet another in a seemingly-endless series of calculated decisions whose only economic logic rests on the eventual, but by no means assured, outcome of a truly excellent wine. He led me to the rows that were to be picked that morning, while his affable Black Labrador snuffled among the vines, gobbling grapes. There had been some rot that year, he explained, and showed me how to spot the withered fruit and cut it out with a pair of harvesting scissors. He was adamant that no tainted fruit should reach the press. Examining each cluster for rot takes that much longer, but the window of picking time remains short, so he had brought in additional hands. Fortunately, he was not counting on the output of mine.

Left to myself, I reached for the first cluster and snipped the stem neatly with the sharp scissors. It lay, compact but substantial, in my hand, the grapes so compressed one into the other that their roundness was actually squared. The fruit was dark purple—almost black—and coated with a ghostly, dusty blush that rubbed off at my touch. I tasted a grape and it was sweet but not overly, and refreshingly juicy. I closed my eyes to savor the flavor, the cool moist freshness of the morning air, the smell of the vines and the cheerful chatter of the pickers.

Each cluster I laid gently into a plastic crate, which I dragged along next to me as I slowly progressed along the row. Under the vines, opportunistic purslane fed off the drip irrigation. Gaby has a benevolent approach to weed control. As he explains it, he'd rather have his vines grow in soil that is alive, vegetated and breathing, than sterilized by herbicides. So he periodically goes through the rows with a special hand-held weeding and tilling machine. And still the weeds appear—just another element to factor in. Instead of pesticides, pheremone-dipped wires twisted around the stakes keep away the grape moths that plague vineyards.

I felt I could stand there, in the pristine mountain air, slipping my hands between the vines to grasp each brilliant cluster, forever. But the sun was rising hot in the sky and the pace picked up as we all rallied to finish one final row. The crates were loaded onto a trailer hitched to Gaby's pickup. One of the pickers, a tall, thin Druze gentleman, passed around little plastic cups of black coffee poured from a thermos. Then they all dispersed.

Gaby unloaded the grapes—about four tons picked that morning—in a chilled storeroom of the former fruit storehouse in the industrial zone of Jish where he makes his wine, a five-minute drive from the vineyard. Within an hour or so, still in their morning chill, the de-stemmed and crushed clusters of grapes would be fed into the pneumatic press for a few hours of maceration, followed by a very gentle pressing. In Gaby's hand, these Barbera grapes were on their way to becoming a light and elegant rosé.

It was early afternoon when I arrived back home, with the feeling that anything that happened the rest of the day would only be an anticlimax. But I'd brought back a chilled bottle of the previous year's rosé that Gaby had given me. It had been rated the best Israeli rosé of the year, and I looked forward to the hour when we would uncork and enjoy it, with a toast to vision and integrity, and to those unique souls who embody them both.

Sukkot in Beit Netufa

You shall live in booths seven days;
all citizens in Israel shall live in booths... Leviticus 23:42

The autumn festival of Sukkot caps off the High Holidays of Rosh Hashanah and Yom Kippur, drawing the observant outdoors and reminding us that the New Year begins in the fall. To fully experience, like the wandering Israelites, what it was like to live without a roof over one's head, Jews are commanded to eat and sleep in the open air for seven days in framed enclosures called sukkot (booths, tabernacles) that are clad in sheets, boards or rushes, and topped with leafy fronds. These makeshift outdoor structures also recall those temporary shelters used by farmers in antiquity to guard over their fields during harvest time, when the fruits of an entire season's work sat ripe and vulnerable, out in the open. Indeed, in yards and porches all over the country, Jewish families celebrate holiday meals and even sleep in their sukkot.

By late September, Sukkot eve, there is very little agricultural activity in the patchwork of agricultural plots that extends across the Beit Netufa Valley. The eggplants, tomatoes, cucumbers, squash, okra, onions, sesame and black-eyed peas have, by and large, run their course, and the dry clods of fallow earth await the first rains of fall.

Improvised guard huts assembled out of salvaged materials are scattered here and there across the expanse of fields to provide shade and shelter to those working the adjacent plots. Only a few weeks ago, families and friends gathered in these modern-day sukkot after an afternoon's weeding and harvesting, passing around small cups of black coffee in the twilight, before returning home for supper. Now, most stand empty and abandoned for the season, tabernacles out of sync with the contemporary celebration.

Driving the rutted dirt road that runs the length of the valley, parallel to the elongated, rectangular plots, Ron and I stopped to take pictures of the various sukkot we encountered. In one sukkah, we found a man sitting by himself, quietly drinking a beer. I told him that I was interested in the sukkot of Beit Netufa. He laughed and said that this was a sukkah of *fellaheen.*

At the edge of one plot, a man dressed in white sat high in a tower-like sukkah, overseeing his wife and two daughters weeding in the rows below. The women smiled shyly, but he refused my request to photograph. Further along, we met a lone farmer walking the rows of his land and asked permission to photograph his well-kept sukkah. He had nothing to hide, he replied, and gave his consent. The cataclysmically hot summer had done no good for his crops, he explained, but the okra and black-eyed peas were still yielding and he was thankful for that. He had even planted cucumbers on the off chance that, this late in the season, *Inshallah*, they might bear fruit.

OLIVES

There is no Jewish olive or Arab olive.

Dr. Shukri Arraf

After the First Rains

*When a person presents an offering of meal to the Lord, his offering shall
be of choice flour; he shall pour oil upon it, lay frankincense on it,
and present it to Aaron's sons, the priests.* Leviticus 2:1

Olives are the last of the summer fruits to ripen, and their harvest,
roughly coinciding with the Jewish New Year, represents the end
of the annual agricultural cycle. The first autumn rainfall not only
washes off the summer dust from the olives and gives them an extra
plumping of moisture before the harvest, but it also softens the
sun-baked earth to ready it for plowing and the sowing of the new
year's grain crop.

If you wait for an olive to ripen completely, after it has turned
from green to black and just before it rots, the bitterness will usually have dissipated just enough to make it edible. Curing them
before they reach this stage, however, yields a nutritious, flavorful
aliment that will last over long periods without spoiling. Yet olives
did not earn their place in the Mediterranean triad because of their
food value.

Long before the culinary art of curing them was ever recorded, olives were cultivated for their oil. In the Biblical texts, there is

scant reference to olives being eaten. Their oil, however—for there was no other oil to speak of at the time—is mentioned numerous times, almost always in a ritual context. The purest oil is used for lighting the lamps of the Temple; oil is mixed with grain and incense as a sacrificial offering; and it is perfumed for anointing prophets and kings.

Olives are small, hard and dense, and don't give up their oil easily. Even when technological innovations in crushing and pressing were introduced around the third century BCE, the production of olive oil was still an intensely laborious process. That, compounded by its great versatility and capacity for storage and transport without spoiling, made olive oil a highly valuable commodity and symbol of abundance, wealth and blessing.

Beyond its sacramental uses, for those who could afford it, olive oil filled a variety of secular functions as well. In addition to fueling lamps, olive oil was used for grooming the skin and dressing the hair, and to soften animal hide clothing and footwear. Wounds were dressed with olive oil infused with medicinal herbs, and it was used for treating ailments. And if any oil was left in the clay storage jar, it went for seasoning, cooking and preserving perishable foods, which, submerged in a bath of oil, were protected against contamination and spoiling. On Balkees's kitchen table there is always a jar of ghostly white spheres of *labaneh* suspended in yellow olive oil, which keeps them fresh for months.

My mother-in-law brought over with her from Romania a deep disregard for olive oil, which she considered to be coarse and too strongly flavored. For every meal she was invited to in our home, we prepared two salads, one with olive oil, and a smaller bowl, just for her, dressed in canola oil. Sometimes, we'd sneak in a dish cooked in olive oil, just to see if she would notice (she invariably did not, or was too polite to mention it). However, when the healthful properties of olive oil became a popular topic on the daytime TV talk shows, she started to come around. As the rest of the Israeli public began to see the olive oil light, commercial cultivation and production of olive oil in this country took off.

In Arab homes, olive oil always was, and continues to be, the main, if not only, oil on the shelf. "*Takhen u zet—amar il beit*" goes the Arabic saying—with flour and olive oil, you have everything a household needs. I once asked Um Malek what she cooks with olive oil, but from her puzzled look, I realized that I needed to rephrase the question. What don't you cook with olive oil? Fried potatoes, she answered. Everything else—the onions for *mejadra*, the greens she gathers on her walks and the okra she picks in the summer— all are ritually immersed in olive oil. No salad, dish of *labaneh* or *hummus* is presentable without first being dressed in fresh green oil. Balkees estimates that her family alone consumes almost 100 liters of oil a year, and not just in the kitchen.

It is common for Arab families in the Galilee to have their own olive trees—with the local Suri variety being the hands-down favorite. Suri olives, whose name is considered to refer to the Lebanese city of Tsur, have an exceptionally high oil content—between 30-38%. Whether picked while still green or black and fully-ripe, and whether cured or pressed for oil, their distinctive fragrance and earthy, slightly-bitter flavor are at the heart of Galilee cuisine.

The gnarled, sculptural aspect of olive trees has much to do with their unique vasculature, in which individual channels, visible almost like veins along the outside of the tree, deliver moisture and nutrients directly from a single set of roots to a corresponding branch. For this reason, an ancient tree will split open over time until it is completely hollow, yet continue to produce fruit. While there are venerable trees believed to be over a thousand years old, gauging their age is almost impossible as there are no rings to count, and the tree propagates from offshoots at its base, ensuring that the same tree will continue to grow even after the fore-bearing trunk has completely decayed and disappeared.

The hardy Suri olive tree thrives in the thin lime and *terra rossa* soils, cool wet winters and long, hot summers of the Galilee, without any special care. An Arab saying compares the olive to the Bedouins, referring to its ability to survive and thrive under only minimal conditions of comfort (the saying goes on to equate the *fellah* to the fig, and the city dweller to the grape, according to their increasing degrees of cultivation).

For the first few years after it is planted, a Suri seedling must be watered, but once its root base is established, the tree grows *baal*, without watering. Indeed, watering a Suri olive tree is considered tantamount to watering down the oil itself. After six to eight years, the tree will begin to bear fruit. It then follows an "alternative bearing" cycle, producing abundantly one year, and sparsely the next. For a family with a grove of trees, the olives they harvest during a year of plenty generally yield oil for an entire year, with enough extra to compensate for the lean year to come.

In Arab communities, the ritual of the harvest once involved the entire extended family, and for those whose olive groves spread across many acres, it could take several weeks. Men took off from their jobs during the olive harvest and schools declared holidays. These days, society is less accommodating. Those families unable to recruit enough workers to complete the picking can let others do the job for them and divide the oil, or in the worst case, leave the fruit to ripen and fall, uncollected, to the ground. Thus, their trees join the ranks of countless others planted in parks, along city streets and in the middle of traffic circles, whose function has declined to the purely aesthetic, and whose fruit has become only seasonal debris that stains the sidewalk.

Olive Harvest in Kfar Reine

And threshing floors shall be piled with grain,
And vats shall overflow with new wine and oil. Joel 2:24

After long months of absence, the reappearance of clouds in the autumn sky is a reason to rejoice, and in Arab villages across the Galilee, a low buzz fills the air. Will there be plentiful olive oil this year? What price will an 18-liter jerry-can fetch? And the question that looms above all others: When are you going to start to pick? Surely not before the first rains...

In the commercial olive-farming sector, these questions are not of great concern. The trees have had their intrinsic fat year/ lean year cycle of fruit yields bred out. Laboratory testing will accurately determine the optimal level of water and oil in the olives to determine exactly when to pick. And the actual harvesting? A mechanical shaker passes through rows of trees planted exactly the right distance from each other to accommodate it. Each tree is given a good shaking, and a shpritz of hormones applied the night before ensures that the fruit will put up no resistance.

Yet in parallel to this high-tech harvesting, families across the Galilee, most but not all Arab, pick their own olives for their own use, in a ritual that has changed little over the millennia.

• • •

When you beat down the fruit of your olive trees,
do not go over them again... Deuteronomy 24:20

When Balkees married Muhammad, according to local custom, she moved to her husband's home, leaving Kfar Reine for Nazareth. But Balkees is a country girl at heart, and when the crush of city life becomes too oppressive, she gets in the family car and makes the ten-minute drive to the village, where her mother, six brothers, three sisters and their families still live. Her siblings' homes are built parallel to one another in a loose family compound, facing and backing a large field planted almost entirely with olive trees. When the time comes to harvest them, Balkees is always there to lend a hand. As the season was approaching, I told her she could count me in as well.

The plan was to start picking after the *Id el Adha* holiday. But then came several days of rain, postponing everything until there were enough sunny days to dry out the mud underneath the trees. It was a weekday morning when I finally joined Balkees and a group of sisters and sisters-in-law in her mother's yard in Kfar Reine. The children were at school and the men at work. Her mother, too old to join in the picking, remained in the house. She had risen early, however, to prepare pita dough and bake *manakish* for the workers.

There were ninety-nine trees to be picked, Balkees informed me, plus one, older and broader than them all, standing next to her mother's home. It was with that tree that we began our work. Actually, we started underneath it. With small pails in hand, we sifted through the slender leaves that blanketed the ground under the tree, plucking out olives that had fallen but were still intact and full of oil. Balkees called this pecking and scrabbling in the undergrowth "chicken work," but I was glad to be joining such a *maadale* effort. The day was beautiful and clear after the rain, and there were plenty of olives to salvage.

The women chatted in Arabic and I managed to follow at least the general themes of the conversation. One of the sisters said she would like to go to Jerusalem that Thursday to pray at the Al Aksa mosque. The others joked that, if she was going to leave them, she'd need to bring two workers in her place. Someone suggested that she could find Sudanese workers in Kfar Manda—where an entire community of North African refugees has sprouted up, drawn by the opportunity for seasonal agricultural work. More jokes followed, and Balkees reminded them that it says in the Koran that all people are equal, regardless of the color of their skin. We are all even, she said, like teeth in a comb.

After we'd picked through the leaves, we spread two large tarps out under the tree and started to pick. These were Suri olives, about the size of fat Jordan almonds, tapering to a point at their tips. According to common custom, it is best to pick for oil when half of the olives on the tree are green and half black. On this day, most of them were black, a sign that we were picking just in time. Left too much longer, they would dry up and drop off the branches and not even the chickens would be interested in them.

Each of us found a spot around the circumference of the tree and started to pick, while Balkees clambered up into the highest branches. With sharp flicks of a thin stick, she sent olives showering down. I reached up into the tree, grabbing the slender branches and pulling downwards to release the fruit straight onto the tarp. Pretend you're milking a goat or a cow, were Balkees' instructions. With each handful of fruit that clattered at my feet, I was reminded of how much I enjoy picking olives. Unlike picking cherries, apples or figs, you are not tempted to pop an olive into your mouth. Olives are all about deferred gratification.

Next to me, one of the sisters-in-law asked me if I liked this kind of work. Very much, I told her. She asked me if I'd done it as a child. I explained that I'd grown up in a city, and that the closest I'd ever come to agricultural work was shopping in the weekend farmer's market. She didn't like olive picking at all, she confided to me. When she was a girl, her parents had never made her help with the olive picking. As a young woman, she'd worked as a clerk in a hospital—a job she clearly remembered fondly. Only after she married and became a housewife was she drafted into the harvest. Now, she was out with us because we were all working right underneath her house and she felt compelled to help. But it's so pleasant, I pointed out, being outdoors on such a lovely day, chatting and joking as we worked. To that she conceded. But she still insisted that it wasn't for her. If she were Balkees, she would never have made the trip.

Once the first tree was stripped of fruit, it was time for a break, with a few sips of black coffee and date cookies. Then we picked up the edges of the tarp, letting all the olives roll to one edge, and one of the sisters loaded them into a sack while the rest of us moved on to the next tree. "*Min ha shajhar el ha hajhar,*" the saying I'd learned from Abu Malek—"from the tree to the stone"—came to mind, with its warning not to delay in getting your fruit to the press. I asked Balkees when the olives we were picking would be taken for pressing, but she explained that they would need to wait for a few more days, spread out on a tarp under one of the houses so they wouldn't spoil. Only then would her brothers have the time to transport the olives to the press in Kfar Kana, just down the road.

After several hours, we had picked only three or four more trees. I asked Balkees how, at that rate, they were ever going to finish ninety-nine trees. First of all, she explained, not all of the trees were so full of olives. And besides, the real work would be done over the weekend when her brothers were home from work. Within a week, she figured, they'd be done.

Various nieces and nephews came home from school and joined us under the trees. The women drifted in and out of their houses. One of them came back with a tray of fresh *manakish*— half of them deep green and shiny with *zaatar* and olive oil and the other half topped with crumbled, salty white cheese. Next to them was a plate with slices of tomatoes and cucumbers. I hadn't realized how hungry I was until the food appeared, and it felt fine to sit in the shade of an olive tree and share in this al fresco meal.

By late afternoon, the workers were still going strong, but I had to leave, parting with wishes of *"ya tiku el affieh"*—that they should have the strength to carry on. I went to say goodbye to Balkees's mother, who had packed up several *manakish* and a plastic soda bottle full of new olive oil for me to take home—pressed from olives picked from another family grove earlier in the season.

On the way home, I thought about my conversation with Balkees's sister-in-law. How easy it was for me to enjoy olive picking when I could join the work and leave it as I pleased. Long after I'd moved on to other tasks, she would probably be working every day until every one of those ninety-nine trees was picked. Harvesting enough olives to produce a year's supply of oil for a large, extended family is onerous work. And as pleasant as the gathering of women under the trees appeared to me, I was well aware of the intrigues and animosities that smoldered under the surface.

In the end, it took about two weeks to finish the job. Some 1400 kilos of olives were picked, yielding about 360 liters of olive oil. No one in the family would need to purchase oil that year. And at almost $7 a liter, this was an effort well spent.

Olives Under Stone

He fed him honey from the crag
And oil from the flinty rock... Deuteronomy 32:13

In the ancient world, there was no material more suitable for extracting oil from olives than stone. One of the earliest systems for producing olive oil, dating back to the Chalcolithic period, around the 4th millennium BCE, involved crushing the fruit in simple bowl-sized basins carved into the bedrock. By the Iron Age, olives were crushed in larger rock-cut basins to release their liquids. But it was during the Hellenistic period, around the 3rd century BCE, that olive processing technology made a spectacular leap forward.

The new generation olive mill featured a round, elevated stone crushing basin and one or a pair of circular millstones. Olives were placed in the basin, and the millstone, affixed to a central axle, rolled round and round, crushing the fruit and pits into a smooth paste. The stone could be pushed by a donkey or a very strong human.

Crushing is only the first in the three-step process for producing olive oil. After that, the olive paste is pressed to extract the liquid—a mixture of water and oil—from the solids. Finally, all that remains is to decant the mixture, allowing the oil to float above the water so that it can be skimmed off the top.

In the classic presses from the Hellenistic era, the olive paste was collected from the crushing basin and placed in porous and flexible, flat-woven baskets. These baskets were stacked one on top of the other and pressure was applied to them using a lever system with a long wooden beam upon which stone weights were suspended (this beam, called a *bahd* in Hebrew, is the origin of the present-day Hebrew term for olive press: *beit bahd*). The liquid oozed through the basket weave and into a clay container set underneath in a specially carved niche. It was a press like this that was discovered at a construction site in Alonei Aba.

What the bulldozer exposed just down the street from my house was the inside of a collapsed cave. Presses like these were generally set up inside caves so that the beams fitted into the crushing basin and the press could be anchored in the walls and ceiling of the cave, and rain wouldn't interfere with the work at hand. In one corner sat the crushing basin, carved out of limestone, about two feet high and twice that across. Next to it were two basalt millstones—one that had presumably been brought to replace the other, which had split into two pieces. Nearby, two parallel stone pillars stood, between which the wooden pressing beam had once been stabilized, and where the baskets of crushed olives were placed. A half dozen stone cubes with holes carved through them like giant square beads had served as weights, suspended on the long-disappeared wooden beam. A cow's jawbone, used to scrape the olive paste out of the basin, was the only other implement found on the site.

There are literally thousands of ancient olive installations across Israel, ranging from simple depressions cut into the stone, to

industrial-scale complexes with numerous presses. In an archaeological survey of ancient olive presses, each one appears as a small
black dot on a map of the country, concentrated in two dense clusters, in the Galilee and the region of Judea. With no other recognition than their mark on the map, the vast majority remains hidden
under the overgrowth on meadows and hillsides, unmarked and
invisible to the public eye. While the installation in Alonei Aba is
a particularly handsome specimen, and was fully documented by
a team of archaeologists from the Antiquities Authority, there are
no funds to maintain or restore it. And so it stands, exposed and
neglected, covered with weeds.

The beam press was replaced by a screw mechanism during the
Roman era, and animal labor for turning the millstones was made
obsolete by motor-driven engines only some 1700 years later. Yet
the millstone-and-basket system can still be found in a few isolated
presses in the Galilee today. The time it takes to produce olive oil
with these presses is relatively long, their output is relatively limited, and the baskets used in the process can never be cleaned well
enough to entirely remove the organic matter, which takes its toll
on the quality of the oil. Ultimately, as the commercial olive oil industry began to grow, and the industrialized olive presses developed
in Europe began to be imported to Israel in the 1980s, stone presses
all but vanished from the landscape.

The new industrial presses are clean and fast and produce yields
unimaginable using the old millstone-and-basket system. With the
option of introducing heat and water into the process, the propor-
tion of oil extracted from the fruit increased radically, but at a cost.
Raising the temperature of the crushed olives loosens the oil mol-

ecules, making them easier to detach from the pulp, yet it also accelerates oxidation and increases acidity. Adding water makes it easier to extract the oil but washes away the health-inducing polyphenols while creating a serious environmental pollutant in the process. Yet this has become the standard price to pay for higher yields.

Of the seventy olive presses located across the Galilee, one can count on one hand those that still crush their olives under stone. One of these is the Rish Lakish olive press in Moshav Tsippori—a homegrown operation of the Noi-Meir family.

*   *   *

Your wife shall be like a fruitful vine within your house;
your sons, like olive saplings around your table. Psalm 128:3

With his billowing white hair and beard, and intense, deep-set eyes, Micha Noy-Meir looks every inch the Biblical patriarch. After years spent farming in Israel and abroad, in 1980, he and his Welsh-born wife Rachelle bought a farm in Moshav Tsippori. They began by raising chickens, then tried their hands at growing medicinal herbs. Today, Micha's expertise is in producing hybrid varieties of vegetables for seeds.

The six Noy-Meir children grew up working on the farm, and each of them has deeply-ingrained environmental sensibilities. As they grew up, however, not one of them could relate to their father's brand of high-tech agriculture. Intent on finding a source of livelihood for them close to home, the Noy-Meir's looked in other directions.

Moshav Tsippori is located just outside of Nazareth, where the dense urban hills give way to rolling agricultural land. Above the moshav, high on a hill, are the excavated remains of an ancient city, now a national park. Considered to be the Roman capital of the Galilee from the 1st century BCE, it had many names: Neronias or Eirenopolis on coins, and Diocaesarea from the time of Hadrian. But it was best known as Sepphoris, presumably after its Hebrew name, Tsippori, so called, according to the rabbis of the time, because it was like a bird (*tsippor*), perched on top of the hill.

From excavations at the site, it is evident that the city's Hellenistic and Jewish residents lived peaceably side by side. During the Jewish revolt against the Romans in 67 CE, the Jewish citizens of the city opted not to participate, and opened the gates of the city to Vespasian, inspiring the minting of coins calling it the "city of peace." In the exquisite mosaics that have been unearthed on the site, one can find Dionysus and Herakles engaged in a drinking contest on the *triclinium* of an elegant villa, and just a few steps away, Abraham preparing to sacrifice Isaac, next to the carriage of the sun god, Helios, depicted on the decorated floor of a synagogue.

During the first centuries of the Common Era, after the expulsion of the Jews from Jerusalem, the Jewish council of the Sanhedrin was temporarily established in Sepphoris, under the leadership of Judah the Prince, redactor of Jewish oral tradition into the Mishnah. An earthquake struck the city in 363, but it was rebuilt and eventually became a significant Byzantine city with numerous churches, sanctified as the birthplace of Mary's mother, Saint Ann. Eventually it was conquered by the Mamelukes, and the hilltop city slid into decline.

At the base of the ancient ruins, closer to the springs and agricultural land, there was a village of Palestinian *fellaheen* called

Seffouri. A convent dedicated to Saint Ann and a school and orphanage were erected on the lower slopes of the hillside, next to the crumbling ruins of a Crusader-era church. In the 1948 War, Seffouri was conquered and razed, its inhabitants seeking refuge in neighboring Arab countries, across the seas, or in nearby Nazareth. On the ruins of the village, a Jewish cooperative agricultural village was established, and named Tsippori.

Towering over the moshav from the top of the hill, a Crusader-era citadel still stands, now an exhibition space and lookout point for visitors to the archaeological site. At the base of the structure, scavenged stone sarcophagi were used as building material, and the different layers of the walls, built by successive conquerors, are distinguishable by the shifts in color and shape of the stone. Nowhere is the layer cake of transient settlement in this contested land, one stratum on top of the other over generations, centuries, and millennia more poignantly evident than here.

Massive, ancient olive trees, some of them many hundreds of years old, can be found growing at the archaeological site and on the hills around the moshav. In Arabic, these formidable old trees are called *romi*, attesting to their great age. Year after year, they give fruit—more if they are pruned and properly tended to, and less if they are neglected—indifferent to who collects it. The Noy-Meir family saw in those trees the opportunity they had been seeking. In a decision that received full consensus across the generations, the family decided to start producing olive oil. They called their olive oil operation "Rish Lakish" after the Jewish gladiator-turned-scholar of Sepphoris, whose spiritual life, described in the Talmud, centered around that very spot.

For the first few years, the Noy-Meir's brought their olives to presses in neighboring villages. But while the flavor of the oil proved to be excellent, they felt they didn't have enough control over the process. Often, the wait for their turn at the press was too long, and the fruit would begin to oxidize, increasing the acidity of the oil to come.

Finally, they decided to purchase their own olive press, and Micha and Rachelle ordered a small, family-sized model from Tuscany. But an olive press needs shelter, and the only available space on their farm was occupied by an old, abandoned chicken coop.

One of the sons offered to take on the project of transforming the broken-down structure into a home for the press. He traveled around the country, meeting and learning from people who specialized in sustainable building. In the end, he decided to rebuild it entirely out of environmentally sound, locally available materials.

First he collected stones and built a low wall that served as the base, or "boots," for the building. On that wall he stacked bales of hay, sewing them together with a long wire "needle." The bales were covered with a mixture of locally-dug clay, ground straw and water. When dry, a first layer of sealant—leftover, inferior-quality olive oil—was rubbed into the earthen surfaces. On top of that, drawing inspiration from Renaissance artists, the walls were brushed with a layer of egg whites as a final sealant. Rachelle remembers buying cartons of eggs in Nazareth, and how the family ate pasta and quiches for weeks.

The structure was fitted with salvaged windows and a massive, old wooden door, and a composting toilet was dug. Outside, a shaded wooden porch now looks out on a yard planted with unruly bushes of lavender, rosemary and mint; close by is Rachelle's organic vegetable garden. Inside, colored glass bottles set into the earthen walls glow blue and green in the sunlight. A corner of the building serves as a visitor's center, with flea market tables and chairs, a massive olive wood counter, and shelves displaying cans and bottles of oil and cured olives. The space is warm and charming, and everything, without and within, is clearly a labor of love.

Even before their Italian press arrived, the Noy-Meirs decided to furnish it with a set of millstones they purchased from a local press that had gone modern. It was simply a matter of taste. Olives crushed under stone, they felt, produced a better-tasting oil. They likened it to the difference between a salad made by slicing lettuce and one made tearing it by hand. Professional olive oil tasters explain that the way olives are crushed exposes different flavors in the oil, and that oil produced under stone tends be fruitier, while the stainless steel blades in most modern presses can leave a bitter, metallic taste.

Every autumn, all six members of the younger generation return from wherever on the globe they happen to be and congregate at the mill. One leads the picking, all of it done by hand. Another is responsible for pruning, and another is in charge of running the press. The eldest daughter, Ayala, handles marketing and sales, and her sister oversees the visitor's center, setting out fresh oil to taste on bite-sized pieces of fresh pita bread to an endless stream of visitors. Cheerful Rachelle flits around like a silver-haired sparrow, minding the grandchildren and preparing meals for the workers, collecting great armfuls of fresh chard and sweet potatoes from the garden.

The same day they are picked, the olives are loaded onto a conveyor belt at the side entrance to the mill, and a roaring blower sends the leaves and sticks flying before the olives are rinsed and spilled into the basin of the press. At the heart of the din, the grindstones spin round and round at a dizzying clip, crushing the olives and their pits into a black paste that resembles tapenade. This dark mash is transferred to a deep stainless steel box fitted with a rotating screw that circulates the crushed olives, separating the drops of oil from the solid matter. A water bath underneath the box enables the temperature of the mixture to be controlled—critical to the quality of the oil; too warm and oxidization proliferates—too cool and the oil will bind to the pulp. A computerized system ensures that the temperature never exceeds 30° Celsius (80° Fahrenheit), well within the limits of "cold pressing" and "extra virgin."

The loosened mixture moves to a centrifuge, which releases the water into one pipe and the oil into another, leaving only a brown, crumbly residue. Unlike most presses, at Rish Lakish, only a minimal amount of water is added to the paste, which ensures that the polyphenols remain in the oil and that the final waste product is almost completely dry. The remaining small quantity of wastewater is fed into a small outdoor pool, planted with papyrus and populated by frogs, in which the residues break down so that it can eventually water the vegetable garden.

Traditionally used as fuel for heating, the solid waste from olive pressing also turns out to be a highly nutritious food for cattle. Because the olive pits at Rish Lakish are crushed and not sliced, there are no sharp pieces that can injure the animals' stomachs, and the local farmers report that the cows eat their olives with relish.

The olive leaves are either packaged as tea for reducing high blood pressure, or carted off to become food for goats.

Every year, Ayala watches over the olive harvest in suspense, waiting to see the flavor, quality and quantity of oil that she will have to sell, and what the price will need to be to make the whole effort worthwhile. Over the years, she has learned some of the less savory aspects of the olive oil business: the illicit mixing of local product with inferior oils, the free use of hormones, and the flooding of the market with imported oil of such poor quality that consuming it is downright unhealthy. At the same time, she has watched as commercial farmers across the country plant thousands of acres of new olive trees, counting on a market that may or may not exist by the time they begin to yield fruit.

The competition is worrisome, but Ayala has regular customers for whom the premium cost is a small price to pay for oil made from organically-grown olives, picked by hand and cold pressed under stone. When the oil is ready, she will start her rounds of deliveries, to restaurants in Tel Aviv, gourmet food stores in Jerusalem and the homes of loyal patrons who buy enough oil to last them through the entire year. Because there are those for whom buying olive oil is not simply a commercial transaction. If they can't grow olives and produce the oil themselves, then they want to know and trust the people who do it exactly the way they would want it done.

The First Oil

You shall further instruct the Israelites to bring you clear oil of beaten olives for lighting, for kindling lamps regularly. Exodus 27:20

In Biblical tradition, the first fruits of the harvest are sanctified, and so it was with olives—not the fruit itself but the oil. Olive oil was produced in pre-Hellenistic presses in two stages. First, the olives were crushed and the oil they yielded was collected. This first pressing, was called *shemen zach katit*—pure beaten oil. After that, hot water was poured onto the crushed olives to extract even more oil. It was the first crushing of oil that was explicitly designated for the lamps of the Temple. These days, olives are pressed in a single round. But receiving the first oil that spills green-gold from the press, out of olives picked with your own hands, feels like nothing less than the fulfillment of a sacred pact.

At any olive press, you can find a dish into which the fresh oil is poured for the clients to taste, with a stack of pita bread for dipping into it. The new oil is cloudy, dense, sharp and aromatic. Like Beaujolais Nouveau, it is fresh, audacious and in your face.

Professional olive tasters have a lexicon to compete with any oenophile. There are desirable traits—fruity, bitter and pungent—

and undesirable ones—fusty, musty, winey and rancid. Tasting apple, artichoke or banana in your oil is a good thing, but bleu cheese, acetone or mud, less so.

At a visit to Rish Lakish while the press was rolling, Ayala offered me some of the fresh oil to taste. It looked, in its small glass bowl, like shiny pea soup. A professional taster had already given it high marks, she told me proudly, but to my untrained palate, the dominant impression was bitterness, followed by an intense burning in the back of my throat. And perhaps a little taste of hay. Bitterness, I was reminded, is a positive attribute and the stinging in the back of the throat, more accurately referred to as pungency, is also positive, as is hay. I took home a five-liter can, and Ron and I poured some over a dish spread with *labaneh*. The oil shone like an emerald pool against a sheet of white satin. Sour, bitter and oh so smooth.

There are those who love the flavor of new oil. But Ayala is quick to caution that it should only be used as a dressing or seasoning, and not for cooking. The dense concentration of solid matter still suspended in fresh oil releases free radicals when heated at high temperatures, which are not so healthy. After three to four months, she assured me, the sediment settles to the bottom, and the clear oil can be used for any manner of cooking. But once it has completely settled, the oil must be separated from the sediment as quickly as possible, otherwise it will begin to oxidize and spoil the oil.

Still, there are some pleasures of fresh oil that must be enjoyed—free radicals or not. In Balkees's house, Muhammad's favorite meal during the season is eggs fried in fresh oil. Or even just fresh pita dipped in oil and salt—simply to savor the flavor "straight up."

At the beginning of the olive season, our friend Akram brought us a plate of Arab cookies called *macarons* that his wife makes every year with the new oil. Shaped like very short cigars, and a comparable deep brown color, they are a delightfully crumbly confection of whole wheat flour, sesame seeds, crushed anise seeds, and, of course, fresh olive oil. After shaping the dough, she rolls each cookie over the mesh of a woven wheat sifter to give them a characteristic bumpy texture.

Nadera's *Macaron* Cookies

Blend 1/2 pound margarine, 1 cup olive oil (fresh if available), 1 cup corn oil, 2 1/2 cups whole roasted sesame seeds, 1 tsp. fresh grated nutmeg, 3/4 cup ground anise seeds, 1 tsp *mahlab* and 2.2 pounds of flour (half white/half whole wheat). Add about 1 cup of water to get a moist dough. Form the dough into long rolls and cut into short little logs. If you want, roll them over a colander or strainer to give them a bumpy texture. Bake at 350° for 15 minutes.

•   •   •

Samuel took a flask of oil and poured some on Saul's head and kissed him, and said, "The Lord herewith anoints you ruler over His own people. 1 Samuel 10:1

I received another warning about fresh oil, this time from Balkees. It should never be used on the skin, she cautioned, as it is too potent. But once it is settled, if any of her children have a cough, she rubs their chest and back with olive oil. And after they were born, she rubbed each child with olive oil from head to toe every day for the first month, to build strength and resistance to illness. I told her that, just as in Biblical times, she was anointing each of her princes and princesses, which made perfect sense to both of us.

The *Journal of Ethnopharmacology* survey of medicinal herbs in Israel, the Golan Heights and the West Bank region reports that practitioners of traditional Arab medicine use olive oil or an olive leaf decoction in various applications to treat coughing, diabetes, high blood pressure and kidney stones, and it is rubbed onto the skin to treat coughing or sore muscles. But olive oil is also the medium used to carry the properties of many of the 129 species listed in the survey. For example. after putting the leaves and stems of rue into a bottle of olive oil and leaving it in the sun for two weeks, the oil can be applied externally to treat backaches, arthritis, skin diseases and eye and ear infections. Fresh purslane juice, mixed with olive oil, can also be applied to the skin to prevent sunstroke.

I have found that when the weather turns cold and the rains disappear for weeks at a time, olive oil comes to the rescue. On those cloudless, bone-dry days, when the sun shines relentlessly and the wind whips brittle and fierce from the east, lips and skin shrivel and hair flies static and erratic. No wonder that the artillery on my bathroom shelf—soap, shampoo, conditioner, moisturizer, body lotion, hand cream and lip balm—are all fortified with olive oil.

Olives Cured in Salt

Verdant olive tree, fair with choice fruit. Jeremiah 11:16

Fifteen years ago, Ron planted a Suri olive tree in our front yard. The sapling was a gift from a friend in Mghrar, a hilltop Arab city overlooking the Sea of Galilee and surrounded by a sea of olive trees. It has thrived in our little parcel of land and grown handsome, expansive and prolific.

Several years ago, we harvested olives to produce oil, and this particular tree contributed generously to the effort. But with oil in our storeroom still left from the previous year, this fall we were harvesting olives only for eating. As soon as the season started, we picked and cured our Suri's green fruit.

Almost two months later, the tree was still laden with olives—all of them now black. The branches were so decoratively strung with ripe fruit, they could have modeled for a Provencal tablecloth. If there ever was a moment to make black olives—when the fruit was still plump and taut, full of moisture from the previous weeks' rains, and just before it started to shrivel and fall to the ground—then this was it.

Green olives and black olives are cured differently. The tradition in these parts when curing green olives is to crack them first—either with a stone or in a special cracking machine—and then to submerge them in salty brine, flavored with garlic, slices of lemon or hot peppers, according to taste. Within a few weeks, the olives are ready to eat. The skin of the green olive can also be pierced with a small slice of a knife, or even left untouched; each system affects the length of time it takes to cure them. A man from Kfar Manda once told me that if you divide your green olives into three groups, cracking the first, slicing the second and leaving the third intact, by the time you've eaten all the cracked ones, the sliced ones will be ready to eat, and when they run out, the intact ones will be ready—until the next year's season.

The riper black olives, however, can be cured in air, salt and sunlight. In Kfar Manda, I had seen black olives Um Malek had spread out on a large stainless-steel tray, sprinkled with salt and left to dry in the sun. This, I decided, would be the system I'd use. I took a bucket and set out to fill it.

It was an overcast morning, cool and grey, with the forecasted rain still distant on the horizon. The hazy white light muted the silvery leaves and the opaque powdering of the olives that rubbed off at my touch. Underneath, the skin was anything but black—more like the midnight purple of the Barbera grapes I'd picked several months earlier. The fruit was remarkably intact, without spots left by piercing insects, or the rot and desiccation of olives past their prime.

When picking olives to produce oil, you can pull the fruit down indiscriminately. Even olives that are dried up like raisins, pocked or bruised all have oil that comes out in the press. But for my purposes, I wanted each fruit to be perfect, so I scanned the slender branches, plucking only the choicest specimens.

Across the nature reserve, the muezzins of Bosmat Tabun began their call to mid-morning prayer—their amplified voices drowning each other out as they intoned their Friday sermons. And then quiet. Just the plunking sound of olives falling into the bucket.

The over-ripe pomegranates left on the nearby tree were split open and baring their crimson hearts, offering up a delectable daily breakfast for the birds. I tried to step lightly—the smashed olives underfoot looked like tiny exploded eggplants. Afterwards, sifting in the undergrowth, I did my chicken work, and topped off the bucket with olives that had fallen under the tree but hadn't yet lost their luster.

The following day, I bought a round stainless steel tray with a low lip, about 3 feet in diameter, in a housewares store in one of the Bedouin villages. These multipurpose trays are standard equipment in any Arab kitchen. I have seen them used for drying herbs and greens, cleaning bulgur, *freekeh* and sesame seeds, and as portable working surfaces on which grape leaves can be stuffed, balls of dough set out and covered with a cloth, and rounds of baked bread stacked to cool. I would be curing my olives on mine.

The only other ingredient I needed was salt. With those perfect purple olives so vivid in my mind, I indulged in an extravagant deviation from the traditional recipe (with a compensatory nod to ancient custom). Even though it was three times the price, I knew only sea salt would do.

After rinsing the olives, I spread them out onto the tray, which neatly accommodated the entire bucketful. In the warm winter sunlight, I systematically sorted through them, picking out any interlopers that were wrinkled or marred, and pulling off the stems. How calming was this quiet, meditative work. I imagined that having tasks like this in one's daily life could keep you sane. Or drive you crazy.

I sprinkled a generous layer of salt over the damp olives and rubbed them until each one had a crusty white coating. As I went to set the tray in the sun, I recognized one serious disadvantage. The average Arab house has a flat roof where foods can safely be left on trays or tarps to dry. With no such protected space, I could only leave my olives on the front porch and hope that no passing animal would develop territorial feelings toward them.

Once the olives were dry and starting to wrinkle—a process that would take several weeks—I would put them in jars and add a little olive oil to coat them. For seasoning, I would add sprigs of rue, that foul-smelling local herb that is the natural partner to black olives.

• • •

Leaving the olives washed, salted and soaking up the sun, Ron and I set off for a walk around the village to see what else was in season. There had been several serious spells of rain that fall and the winter growth was already a vibrant and exhilarating presence. Great bunches of *hubeisa* waved like green banners by the roadside, and in the plowed fields, tender shoots of wheat were already spreading a downy, verdant veneer over the darkened earth.

In one of the natural oak groves still left standing behind a new neighborhood, we checked the asparagus bushes, but they had still not put forth any shoots. There was a sudden crashing of dried leaves and sticks, and a wild boar, scared out of its hiding place, tore off to find another cover. Boars are the largest wild mammal left in this region, and this one was bristly and tusked; about as tall as a German shepherd and several times as stout, it was remarkably speedy on its short legs.

On the edge of a wheat field, we found a freshly-emerging bunch of wild spinach. The leaves were still too small to pick, but I made a mental note of the spot to return with my kitchen knife and a bag in another week.

We headed up through the dairy and back onto the streets of the village. In the yards of the older neighborhoods, citrus trees hung loaded with fruit—grapefruit, oranges and clementines. Underneath them lay more fruit, rotting in the wet grass. Looking for a reason for all this waste, Ron explained to me that the fruit wasn't any good. The clementines were the size of ping-pong balls, leathery and dry. I picked a decent-sized orange, peeled off a piece of skin and tasted the inside with the tip of my tongue. Horribly sour. Many of the trees had been planted by Ron's parents' generation, he told me, and they were simply old. They also did not receive enough water; with the price of water these days, who could afford to water all of these trees?

We ourselves have long since stopped watering our yard, and only when the rains call up the natural winter growth do we enjoy anything resembling a lawn. But the olive trees thrive, as do the pomegranates and the fig trees, surviving purely on the water that the unique ecosystem of the Galilee provides. Growing *baal*.

Balkees told me she had read that *baal* agriculture actually refers to the ancient fertility god *Baal*, worshiped by the Canaanites and described in the Bible. It certainly seems plausible—particularly when the authenticity of matters like this generally rests somewhere between historical provenance and faith. And in the agricultural world, hasn't faith been the wild card in a farmer's hand ever since the first stone Venus was planted in a crop row?

These days, the drama of the early rains and the late plays itself out largely to an oblivious audience. But I have found good company among those for whom the appearance of clouds on the horizon or the discovery of a tender shoot of *luf* is an answer to their prayers.

Finding my own place within the exquisite balance of the seasons and the plants—both cultivated and wild—that sustain us each in their time, fills me with the wonder and awe that has moved people here for millennia. The Galilee is my home, and for this I am grateful.

Inshallah

If several days go by in which Balkees and I don't see each other, we like to talk on the phone. We tell each other our dreams and then analyze them. We discuss what is on the stove and what is in the oven. What her children are up to, and mine. Her husband, and mine. Plans for our next excursion.

In one of these evening conversations, she asked me a question. "And I want you to answer me honestly," she said. "After knowing me for all this time, have you started to see the world through my eyes?"

I only had to think for a second before I told her that yes I did. "And do you find that you see the world through my eyes?" I asked.

"Yes, I do," she answered. "How blessed we are," she said, "that we met that day. It was the hand of God."

"And how much each of us has changed since then," I replied. "And I hope we can continue to change and grow together."

"*B'ezrat hashem*—God willing," she said.

And I answered "*Inshallah.*"

Glossary of Arabic Terms

Baal: Agriculture that relies only on rainwater and dew

Batikh el Batof: Watermelon from the Bet Netufa Valley

Bustan: Fruit orchard and garden

Dibes: Syrup made of long-cooked fruit, i.e. figs, grapes

Diwan: Central salon or seating area in an Arab home

Elsaina: An edible wild plant from the sage family

Freekeh: Wheat that has been harvested while still green, and then roasted over a fire. Served in soup, or as a side dish, like rice.

Ftayir: baked triangles of dough filled with spiced leafy greens

Hafla: Festive meal

Hakura: Vegetable garden

Hilayon: Wild asparagus

Hubeisa: Mallow, an edible wild plant

Ibrahim Avinu: Abraham the Patriarch

Jarjir ha nahal: Wild cress

Jibni: Firm, salty white cheese made of sheep or goat milk

Katayef: Traditional Ramadan dessert of syrup-soaked pancakes folded over a chopped walnut and cinnamon mixture or jibni

Keffiye: Traditional headdress worn by Arab men

Leben: Yoghurt, often made of sheep or goat milk

Labaneh: Smooth, creamy white cheese made of leben

Malukhiya: The jute plant, whose green leaves are used to make thick soup.

Manakish: Pita bread spread with zaatar mixture, moistened with olive oil, and baked.

Muni: A *fellah's* inventory of grains, olive oil and other comestibles

Saada: Bitter/sour black coffee that is cooked for long hours and served to guests

Selek: Edible wild spinach leaves

Shoraba: Soup

Sulkha: Peace agreement to resolve a conflict, usually between clans

Wadi: Water course between two hills or mountains, usually dry in the summer.

Zaatar: An edible wild plant of the *Labiatae* family, including varieties of oregano, marjoram and thyme. Also the name given to the popular spice mixture, composed of dried zaatar leaves, sumac, sesame, olive oil and salt.

Zalabiya: Balls of fried dough, soaked in honey

Made in the USA
Charleston, SC
02 May 2012